Advance praise for Joseph Califano's *How to Raise a Drug-Free Kid*

"Teens and college students are surrounded by drugs and alcohol, in school, at play, even at home. As a physician specializing in adolescents, I know that since they have to deal with this problem, then as a parent so do you. *How to Raise a Drug-Free Kid* provides the practical advice and information that every parent needs. If you read only one book, this is the one."

—Ralph I. Lopez, MD, clinical professor of pediatrics, Weill Cornell Medical College and author of *The Teen Health Book: A Parents' Guide to Adolescent Health and Well-Being*

"A parent's toolbox for today. An invaluable primer to help you help your children navigate the difficult and contradictory messages about drugs and alcohol."

—Jamie Lee Curtis, mother, actress, and author of children's books

"A must read for all parents to learn new ways to help their children grow up safe and drug free. Through its 9 facets of parental engagement, Joseph Califano's *How to Raise a Drug-Free Kid* gives parents proven, practical ways to constructively engage in the lives of their children and to use their 'Parent Power' in order to be their child's strongest positive influence."

—Chuck Saylors, president, National PTA

"Numerous studies show both the influence parents can have on their teens' behavior and the problems they have in exerting it. This wise, practical and well written book gives them the tools they need. I enthusiastically recommend it to parents."

—Herbert D. Kleber, MD, professor of psychiatry and director, Division on Substance Abuse, Columbia University and New York State Psychiatric Institute

ALSO BY JOSEPH A. CALIFANO, JR.

How to Raise a Drug-Free Kid

THE STRAIGHT DOPE
FOR PARENTS

JOSEPH A. CALIFANO, JR.

Founder and Chair
of The National Center on
Addiction and Substance Abuse at Columbia University

A Fireside Book
Published by Simon & Schuster
New York   London   Toronto   Sydney

Fireside
A Division of Simon & Schuster, Inc.
1230 Avenue of the Americas
New York, NY 10020

First Fireside trade paperback edition August 2009

FIRESIDE and colophon are registered trademarks of Simon & Schuster, Inc.

For information about special discounts for bulk purchases,
please contact Simon & Schuster Special Sales at
1-866-506-1949 or business@simonandschuster.com.

The Simon & Schuster Speakers Bureau can bring authors
to your live event. For more information or to book
an event contact the Simon & Schuster Speakers Bureau at
1-866-248-3049 or visit our website at www.simonspeakers.com.

Designed by Elliott Beard

Manufactured in the United States of America

3   5   7   9   10   8   6   4

Library of Congress Cataloging-in-Publication Data
Califano, Joseph A.
How to raise a drug-free kid : the straight dope for parents / by Joseph A. Califano.
p. cm.
"A Fireside Book."
1. Substance abuse—United States—Prevention. 2. Parenting—United States.
I. Title.
HV4999.C45C34   2009
649'.48—dc22   2009007178

ISBN 978-1-4391-5631-5
ISBN 978-1-4391-6636-9 (ebook)

*For the families that have endured the agony
of a child addicted to drugs or alcohol
with the hope and prayer that this book
will help other families avoid such tragedies
and
For the newest Califano grandchild, Grace Frances Becker*

The author is donating all royalties
from sales of this book to
The National Center on Addiction and Substance
Abuse at Columbia University.

Contents

Preface

Parents, if you had a crystal ball and could see your child's future, what would you want to see?

You'd want to see your child healthy, productive, and fulfilled, wouldn't you?

Every day, you work hard to be a good parent, doing hundreds of things to make that future come true for your child. But sometimes it's hard to know if all the big and little things you do make any difference.

What if I could tell you which parenting actions work?

What if I could tell you what specific things you can do to teach, protect, and empower your child to have the greatest chance of making that future come true?

Well, in this book I'm about to do just that.

Since 1992, The National Center on Addiction and Substance Abuse at Columbia University—popularly called CASA—has been surveying teens and parents, talking to families, interviewing the best researchers, pediatricians, adolescent counselors, scientific experts, clergy of every faith, school nurses, teachers, and principals, studying the successes and failures of schools, parents, families, and teens with one objective: to find the most effective ways to raise drug-free children.

We've learned that raising healthy, drug-free kids is first and foremost a Mom-and-Pop operation, that your Parent Power is the key.

And we've learned that steering your kids away from alcohol and drug use will not only help give them a healthy childhood, it will also set them on the road to a healthy, productive, satisfying, and happy life as adults.

Why?

Because nearly two decades of CASA research demonstrate that a child who gets through age twenty-one without smoking, abusing alcohol, or using illegal drugs is virtually certain never to do so.

This book is designed to help you help your kids get through the formative years drug free.

I know how important this is to you because we at CASA receive so many calls and e-mails from parents for advice about how to help their sons and daughters negotiate that dangerous decade from ten to twenty-one without getting into alcohol and drugs or getting hooked on cigarettes.

We've learned from interviewing thousands of teens that they see drugs as the number one problem they face. And we've learned from talking to thousands of parents that their worst nightmare is that their child will become hooked on alcohol or illegal drugs, or suffer the devastating consequences of an auto accident or sexual assault as a result of a friend's alcohol or drug abuse.

Every American child will be offered alcohol, cigarettes, addictive prescription pills, marijuana, other illegal drugs, or a number of these substances before they graduate from high school. Many will get such offers while in middle school. And most will get such offers on numerous occasions.

This book will give you the tools to prepare your daughter or son for that moment of decision when a friend, a classmate, or a group at a party offers them a drink, a joint, a snort, or a pill to get high. It will give you the Parent Power to develop in your children the will and the skills to make healthy choices.

As a parent, you are the most influential source of information your child has. Talking to your child about smoking cigarettes, drinking alcohol, and using other drugs is what's most likely to make a difference in whether your child gets into these things. Teenagers who learn about the risks of drugs from their parents are much more likely never to try them. So don't rely on your child's school, or some program, or anyone else to educate your children about the dangers of substance abuse.

You are the messenger that your children are likeliest to listen to.

The message to give your children about smoking and illegal drugs is straightforward: "No. Never." The message to give your children about alcohol is more complex: "No. Never for persons under twenty-one. Never for some others like alcoholics and those with a genetic predisposition to alcoholism. But yes, in moderation, for other adults who wish to drink."

When you talk to your children about alcohol, cigarettes, and other substances, it is important that you feel comfortable and know what you're talking about. Teenagers will ask tough questions; they'll challenge you. You don't have to become a psychopharmacologist or substance abuse expert, but you do need to know enough to handle questions and challenges like:

- "You and Dad drink wine/beer/a martini with dinner. Why can't I?"
- "What's the difference between your drinking beer and my smoking pot?"
- "So long as I don't drink and drive, what's wrong with having a few beers at a party? All the other kids do."
- "Prescription drugs are safe. What's so bad about using them at a party?"
- "How could marijuana be bad for you if it's just a natural herb?"
- "Lots of kids on the football/basketball/soccer team/honor roll drink and smoke pot and they're fine."

- "Most kids who smoke cigarettes don't smoke pot, and most kids who smoke pot don't turn into drug addicts. I can handle it. Don't be so uptight."

This book will give you the tools to answer questions and challenges like these, and to deal with the distortions kids will hear from friends, movies, and music around them. The insights and information on these pages will give you the confidence to speak to your children comfortably and persuasively, with love and authority, about the dangers of adolescent drug, alcohol, and tobacco use. They will give you the tools to set clear and realistic expectations for your children about substance use, to know what to do if you discover your child is experimenting, and to recognize when your child (and you) might need professional help.

You'll learn why any drug use can open the door to future problems and heavier drug use. You'll see how drugs are particularly perilous for adolescents because their brains are still developing. You'll get the facts—a cold and true picture—about the substances teens are likeliest to use: cigarettes, alcohol, marijuana, and prescription drugs. At the end of the book, there's a "Parent Power Glossary for Parents and Teens" with detailed information about drugs like inhalants, DXM, OxyContin, ecstasy, and methamphetamine, what each drug looks like, how it works, what symptoms it causes, and how dangerous it is. You can refer to this glossary, alone or with your teen, to learn more about specific drugs.

There are no silver bullets and there is no such thing as perfect parenting. Even the finest parents may end up suffering the anguish and pain of seeing a child become addicted to drugs or dying from alcohol poisoning in a college hazing incident. But parents have greater power than anyone else to reduce or eliminate those risks for their children.

For many parents, teen substance abuse is the boogeyman under the bed—something they fear and hope will never happen. This leads some parents to shut their eyes, pull up the covers, and hope for the best. But ignoring the threat of teen substance abuse or assuming there's no threat to *your* child won't make it go away. Your disengagement will simply leave your child alone to navigate the treacherous rapids of tobacco, alcohol, and illegal and prescription drugs without a parental compass to guide them.

At CASA we have no cultural agenda, no political leaning, no drug war to defend, no drug war to attack. We work hard to identify the most practical, realistic ways to help parents raise their children drug free. This may seem a daunting task in twenty-first-century America. But I know you can do it and I am convinced that this book will be an invaluable tool to help you use your formidable Parent Power to nourish in your children the will, skills, and strength to choose not to use.

PART I

PREVENT IT

1

TAKE A HANDS-ON APPROACH TO PARENTING

As a parent you have the greatest power to influence your children—even your teenage children. You have more power than any law, any peer pressure, any teacher or coach, any priest, rabbi, or minister, any music, film, or Internet site, any rock star, movie star, or famous athlete, even any sister, brother, aunt or uncle.

You have the power to empower your children to make good choices—sensible, healthy choices—throughout their teen years. The key to this power—what I call Parent Power—is being engaged in your children's lives.

Parental engagement isn't rocket science. It's hands-on parenting. It's relaxing with your kids, having frequent family dinners, supervising them, setting boundaries, establishing standards of behavior, getting interested in their school, friends, and social activities, loving and disciplining them, being a good role model.

Why is parental engagement so important? Because children of hands-on parents are far less likely to smoke, drink, or use other drugs.

Why is it so important to keep your teenager from doing these things? Because a child who gets through age twenty-one without smoking, abusing alcohol, or using illicit drugs is virtually certain to *never* do so. And that child is much likelier to have a healthy, happy, and productive life.

During childhood and adolescence, using alcohol and other drugs can interfere with your child's physical, emotional, and cognitive development. We know a lot more today about the dangers of smoking, drinking, and drug use than we did in the past. The scientific evidence is now overwhelming that teen alcohol and drug abuse interferes with brain development and can inflict serious, sometimes irreversible, brain damage in the long term. Even in the short term, such abuse adversely affects the brain, reducing a teen's ability to learn and remember, processes critical to children in school.

The earlier and more often an adolescent smokes, drinks, or uses illegal drugs, the likelier that adolescent is to become addicted. Adolescents are more sensitive than adults to the addictive properties of cigarettes, alcohol, and drugs like marijuana, OxyContin, and cocaine. Every day, every month, every year that your child goes without taking that first puff, sip, hit, or pill decreases the likelihood that your child will become addicted, develop related mental or physical illnesses as a result of substance abuse, or suffer the tragic consequences of a substance-related accident.

Through your engagement, you can influence, teach, encourage, correct, and support your children so that they develop the will and the skills to say no to tobacco, alcohol, and other drugs. Indeed, your Parent Power is the most effective instrument in the substance-abuse-prevention toolbox.

In this book I give you some effective, straightforward substance-abuse-prevention techniques that are what the experts call "evidence-based"—that is, supported by scientific analysis and evaluation. I'll describe these tools and how they work.

Communication doesn't start when your child is seventeen; it should start when your child is three. So by the time that your child is seventeen, there's a pattern of communication that has hopefully been going on for some time.

Dr. Ross Brower, deputy medical director of the Adolescent Development Program, Weill Cornell Medical College

My focus is preventing substance abuse among tweens (ages 8–12) and teens (ages 13–19), but the parental engagement I encourage begins even earlier and extends through the college years.

Establishing a strong connection and good communication with your kids will become more difficult if you wait until the teen years, when children become more independent. The communication foundation you set early in your child's life will be invaluable during the turbulent teens.

THE NINE FACETS OF PARENTAL ENGAGEMENT

Parenting is an art, not a science. Being engaged in your children's lives doesn't require being a supermom or superdad. It simply means using your strengths and taking advantage of opportunities to be a good parent.

Like a brilliantly cut diamond, parental engagement has many facets. Think of the nine facets of parental engagement as an action guide for good parenting. If they seem intuitive to you, that's great! It means you're already on the right track.

The Nine Facets of Parental Engagement

1. Be there: Get involved in your children's lives and activities.
2. Open the lines of communication and keep them wide open.
3. Set a good example: Actions are more persuasive than words.
4. Set rules and expect your children to follow them.
5. Monitor your children's whereabouts.
6. Maintain family rituals such as eating dinner together.
7. Incorporate religious and spiritual practices into family life.
8. Get Dad engaged—and keep him engaged.
9. Engage the larger family of your children's friends, teachers, classmates, neighbors, and community.

With these nine facets of parental engagement, you will have the tools to create a relationship that will enable you to raise your children to be healthy and substance free, poised to develop their talents to the fullest. The benefits of such a relationship reach well beyond substance-abuse prevention. But without this foundation, your admonitions to say no to drugs and alcohol will be like trees falling in an empty forest: Your children will not hear them, much less be influenced by them.

1. Be There: Get Involved in Your Children's Lives and Activities

Being there—being physically and emotionally available and present—is the essence of parental engagement.

There are endless casual opportunities to be there: eating dinner together as a family, celebrating birthdays and holidays, helping your sons or daughters with their homework, going to their athletic events, school plays, and debates, attending religious services together, taking walks, watching television, going to the movies, fishing, hunting, shopping, driving. These moments are all opportunities for talking and listening to your children about all kinds of things. They are situ-

I am a big advocate of playing with your kids (Monopoly, card games, puzzles) and sports (catch, soccer, baseball). The family that plays together stays together.

Jeanne Reid, mother of three children

ations where you can comfortably help your children learn to make healthy, sensible decisions.

As a parent, you are likely to see your children's strengths and weaknesses before they do, and you can reinforce their strengths and help them to deal with their weaknesses by praising them for their efforts and encouraging them to strive for success. Parental praise, affection, acceptance, family bonding, and discipline are all associated with reduced risk of substance abuse. Such parental support nourishes a confidence in children that their families are sufficiently strong and durable to cope with stressful life events. That confidence is tied to a reduced risk of substance abuse.

Being there, being physically and emotionally present, means being sensitive to the complex biological, emotional, psychological, neurological, and hormonal transitions your kids are experiencing. The tween and teen years involve many difficult transitions and challenges that have an impact on your child's self-esteem, confidence, and feelings of self-worth.

Especially during the tween and teen years, your children confront a confounding array of issues about their beliefs, values, sexual activity, entertainment, friends, and cliques, as well as tobacco, alcohol, and drug use. At these vulnerable and formative ages, they do not yet have the emotional maturity and brain development to control their impulses or to sort out their options and make sound choices on their own. They may often be reluctant to admit it, but they both need and want your help to avoid making impulsive mistakes. Although your children will try to assert their independence, they want you close enough to catch them when they fall, soothe them when they feel hurt, and hug them when they're scared or ashamed.

Being there pays off big time: Teens who say they have an excellent relationship with their parents are less likely to smoke, drink, or use drugs. So are teens who grow up in caring and supportive family environments, where parents have high expectations of their children and welcome their children's participation in family routines and rituals.

So be there—at school and family events, dinner, and religious services—and see what a difference it makes for your teen.

2. Open the Lines of Communication and Keep Them Wide Open

Too many parents assume that they are the last people on earth their teens want to talk to about their problems. How many times have we heard "My fourteen-year-old daughter cringes when I come near her to talk about her life" or "My sixteen-year-old son will never open up to me about issues like drugs or parties"?

That's not necessarily true. And even if you expect to get such a reaction from your child, simply expressing your interest in your child's life is helpful.

Every year at CASA we survey teens from across the nation. Without exception, in response to an open-ended question, the lion's share of teens tell us that drugs are their top concern. Yet more than one-third of teens have never had serious discussions with their parents about the dangers of drug use, and only a quarter have had in-depth conversations with their parents about the dangers of prescription drug abuse. Many teens who haven't had those conversations wish they could honestly discuss substance abuse with Mom and Dad.

Children who learn about the risks of drugs from their parents are much less likely to use them. Most girls and many boys credit conversations with Mom and Dad as their reason for deciding not to do drugs.

Your children are likely to care more about what you think than anything else they see or hear. Indeed, teens consistently tell us that "disappointing their parents" is a key reason that they don't use drugs. Signaling your disapproval by sending your children a clear message not to use substances may be the difference between your teen saying no when offered opportunities to smoke, drink, or use drugs and your teen trying these substances.

Teens—even older teens—may not know how to ask for your help. It may be difficult for them to be forthcoming, but they look to you for advice, encouragement, and support. These conversations may be hard for you too. Talking to your child or teenager openly about issues like substance abuse may feel uncomfortable, or you may be unsure about what to say. In the next chapter, I offer plenty of tips on how to make those conversations comfortable and productive.

3. Set a Good Example: Actions Are More Persuasive than Words

The most important facet of parental engagement is your own conduct. Your kids will be more affected by what they see you do than what they hear you say. Moms and Dads who smoke cigarettes, abuse

---

If you don't want them to drink . . . but the message is, "This is what Mommy does every single night" . . . when they go out into the world it's not going to be so foreign for them to say, "My mom drinks every night. I can drink every night." It really has to do with practicing what you preach.

Jamie Lee Curtis, actress and author of a series of children's books, who lived with the alcohol and drug abuse of her movie-star parents, Janet Leigh and Tony Curtis, and later experienced her own alcohol and Vicodin addiction

---

"Yes, but Mummy and Daddy are on legal drugs."

alcohol, smoke marijuana, and use drugs are likelier to have kids who smoke cigarettes, abuse alcohol, smoke marijuana, and use drugs.

Parental drinking behavior can decisively shape a child's view of alcohol use, even at the earliest ages. Dr. Stanley Gitlow, one of the nation's premier alcoholism clinicians, tells me, "When Dad comes home after work and rushes to belt down a couple of martinis, by the time his baby is three years old, that tot sees drinking as a way to relax. Years later, when that child starts bingeing on the weekends in high school, he won't even know that he picked it up watching Dad hit the martinis more than a decade before."

You don't have to be a teetotaler to be a good role model. There's a difference between rushing to belt down martinis every night and having some wine with dinner.

Even if your own behavior is not perfect, setting a healthy example and changing your behavior sends an influential message to your children. For example, if you are a smoker, the younger your children are when you quit smoking, the less likely they are to smoke at all. Being honest about your struggles and inviting your children to witness and support your efforts to stop smoking will empower your children to resist smoking in the first place and to quit themselves if they start.

4. Set Rules and Expect Your Children to Follow Them

Engagement in your children's lives involves establishing expectations and limits. It means setting curfews and checking ahead with hosts of parties your teens want to attend to make sure a chaperone is present and alcohol is not. It means monitoring your children's Internet activities, the movies they see, the concerts they attend, and the video games they play. It means enforcing consequences for stepping beyond the boundaries you set.

You can expect your kids to argue about almost every line you draw. They'll say the curfew is too early, that their friends can stay out a lot later. They'll argue that they are old enough to go out without telling you where they are going. They'll claim you're embarrassing them by calling other parents to make sure those parents will be home for the teen party at their house and that alcohol won't be served or allowed. They'll tell you that every fifteen-year-old sees R-rated movies. They'll resent what they insist is an invasion of their privacy when you restrict their Internet activities. And they'll say that other kids can buy M-rated games no matter how much violence, sex, or drugs are in them, and that other kids' parents let their children go to any concert. Their common chorus will be, "All my friends can do it" or, "Don't worry, I can handle it" or, "Don't you trust me?"

During our teen focus groups at CASA, I've heard all those arguments. But when I draw out teens, more often than not they admit that the rules their parents establish show that "My parents really care about me." Your children need and deserve guidance, information, supervision, and discipline. Children aren't born knowing how to set their own boundaries. The rules you establish, the lines you draw, and the messages you send become your children's internal compass for their own behavior.

Children look to you not only to set clear rules, but also to enforce them fairly. Enforcing the rules, through punishment or other consequences, is an essential exercise of your Parent Power and a key lesson in your children's learning process.

Your children will appreciate and respect the rules you craft—not going to parties where alcohol is served, setting curfews and restrictions on movies or video games—if they understand the reasons behind those rules and if the rules are consistently enforced. Answer their inevitable "Why" questions. Here's a sample exchange:

Teen: "Why are you spoiling my fun when everyone else is doing it?"

Parent: "It's dangerous, illegal, and unhealthy for fifteen-year-olds

---

Jane Hambleton of Fort Dodge, Iowa, bought her nineteen-year-old son an Oldsmobile Intrigue. She set two firm rules: no booze, and always keep the car locked. Three weeks later, Jane found a bottle of booze in the car. Her son said that he was the designated driver and that a friend had left the bottle in the car. Jane believed her son, but thought that her son needed to learn a lesson about rules and consequences—she took the car away and sold it. The ad she ran in the *Des Moines Register* read: "OLDS 1999 Intrigue. Totally uncool parents who obviously don't love teenage son, selling his car. Only driven for three weeks before snoopy mom who needs to get a life found booze under front seat. $3,700/offer. Call meanest mom on the planet."

Connie Schultz, *Chicago Sun Times*, January 17, 2008

to be at parties where alcohol is served. The possible consequences—drunk driving, aggressive sexual advances, alcohol poisoning—are not something I want you exposed to. It's not that I don't trust you, it's that I know how easily things can get out of hand if kids are drinking."

If you explain the logic behind the rules and limits, it will help your children tap into that logic when they are faced with tough decisions, and to exert self-control in the face of inevitable temptations.

To the extent possible, the consequences for breaking the rules should be laid out in advance. This way, children know what to expect if they push the limits, and will be more likely to accept the consequences as fair. Another advantage of advance notice is this: When your child breaks the rules, you can focus on what caused the behavior and how to make sure it won't happen again, rather than arguing about the punishment.

Do you want to know one of the things kids criticize most about parents? Inconsistency. Kids respect and need parents who set rules and stick to them. Kids are rather unimpressed with the parents who bend the rules every time their kid complains. In one CASA teen focus group, a teen told me about an incident in which the high school principal enforced a rule that punished kids caught smoking pot by prohibiting them from attending the senior prom. The students' parents lobbied and the principal reversed his decision. The other kids in the school said they had no respect for the indulgent parents who pressured the school to change the rules for their kids, or for the principal who caved in to the pressure.

Keep in mind that children will often test your limits: It's a normal part of growing up. When your children break the rules you set, be careful to judge the *act*, not the *child*. When parents judge children as "stupid," "worthless," or "bad," it can reinforce the bad behavior because the children may learn to think of themselves that way. When parents focus on *why* the behavior was unacceptable, children learn how to make better choices in the future.

We learned a lesson in consistency from our thirteen-year-old daughter. She was invited to a summer-camp reunion in Greenwich Village, a bus ride away. We agreed on condition that she would call us to let us know she arrived safely. We assumed she'd call by 8 P.M., but she didn't until 10 P.M. We were worried sick. She wanted to know, "Am I in trouble?"

A half hour later she came home, apologized, and asked the consequences. She didn't accept her month grounding easily, "Just because I forgot to call!"

A week later she was invited to attend a high school drama-society meeting, a great honor for a middle-school student. We were caught between the grounding and the special event. I came up with the Monopoly concept of a "Get Out of Jail" card. I drew up a "Get Out of One Grounding Free" card for use at the bearer's discretion.

"You were grounded, but we know the high school drama club is important, so we give you a choice to use the card."

To our astonishment, she said, "I can't take this. I don't like being grounded and I think it's unfair, but if you go back on this, I won't ever know when you mean things. Thanks, but no thanks."

Dr. Ralph Lopez, pediatrician and author of
*The Teen Health Book: A Parent's Guide to
Adolescent Health and Well-Being* (2003)

5. Monitor your Children's Whereabouts

Supervision serves a purpose. Adolescents who are closely supervised by their parents are much less likely to smoke, drink, or use drugs.

Simply realizing that they are being monitored, that their parents insist on knowing where they are and who they are with, may deter children from doing these things.

In a 2008 survey CASA found that about half of twelve- to seventeen-year-olds typically go out on school nights (Monday through Thursday) to hang out with friends, and that most of their parents seem unaware of where their children are and what they're up to. This spells trouble. The later teens are out with friends on a school night, the likelier it is that those friends are drinking or doing drugs. Half of teens who come home after 10:00 P.M. on a school night report that drug and alcohol use was going on among their friends, as do almost a third of kids who come home between 8:00 P.M. and 10:00 P.M. on a school night.

Getting to know your child's whereabouts after school and on weekends gets you in position to make sure they're occupied appropriately, to move to prevent risky situations and, if necessary, to intervene in time to help them. There is an important corollary to Grandma's adage about idle hands being the devil's workshop: Teens left alone to fend for themselves for extended periods of time are at greater risk for getting drunk and getting high.

6. Maintain Family Rituals, Such as Eating Dinner Together

Dinner makes a difference.

More than a decade of CASA research has consistently found that the more often children have dinner with their parents, the less likely they are to smoke, drink, or use drugs. This chart, based on CASA's surveys, tells the story dramatically:

Percentage of 12- to 17-Year-Olds Who Have Used Substances

	0–2 family dinners/week	5–7 family dinners/week
Alcohol	47%	30%
Cigarettes	26%	10%
Marijuana	25%	8%
Prescription Drugs	7%	2%
Other Drugs	7%	2%

CASA. The Importance of Family Dinners IV (2007)

Family dinners are so important that I have devoted an entire chapter to the subject, Chapter 3, "Eat Meals Together—Dinner Makes a Difference." I also discuss other family rituals—celebrating birthdays, holidays, and family events—which are excellent examples of comfortably exercising your Parent Power.

7. Incorporate Religious and Spiritual Practices into Family Life

Religion can benefit your children immeasurably. Whatever your religion—Buddhist, Catholic, Hindu, Jewish, Mormon, Muslim, Protestant, or if you simply define yourself as spiritual—sharing your faith with your children will reduce the likelihood that they will abuse harmful substances. Teens who consider religion to be an important part of their lives are far less likely to smoke, drink, or use drugs.

Faith is an effective substance-abuse-prevention tool because it offers people, including children, strength in the face of adversity.

Those who are involved in their church are much less likely to be involved in drugs.

Michael J. Sheehan, archbishop of Santa Fe, New Mexico

Percentage of 12- to 17-Year-Olds Who Have Used Substances by Religious Service Attendance

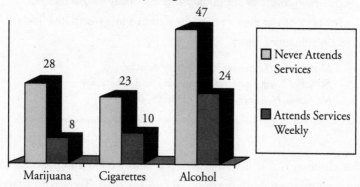

CASA. National Survey of American Attitudes on Substance Abuse XIII: Teens and Parents (2008)

People who are spiritual or make religious practice a part of their lives derive strength and support from the religious community that surrounds them, from the teachings of their faith, and if they believe in a higher power such as God, from that higher power. With these resources, they don't need to turn to alcohol and drugs for relief.

For you and your children, religion can be a meaningful resource for morals and values. When you explain to your children why they shouldn't abuse substances, your religion may provide some valuable teachings. In most religions, including Judeo-Christian traditions, the body and mind are sacred. Abuse of alcohol, tobacco, and other drugs should be avoided because they harm the body and degrade the individual's dignity. The Catholic Church teaches that we are all made in God's image and with free will, characteristics incompatible with substance abuse and addiction. In Islam, alcohol and other intoxicants are forbidden because they make the body and mind impure. In the philosophy of Buddhism, alcohol and drugs are shunned because they cloud the mind, which can incite further improper behavior.

Another tangible benefit of sharing your religious practice with

> People who are actively involved in religious practices or
> have high levels of spirituality are less likely to use alcohol,
> use tobacco—if they smoke, they smoke less—and less likely
> to be substance users.
>
> Margaret A. Chesney, PhD, deputy director,
> National Center on Complementary and Alternative
> Medicine, National Institutes of Health (NIH)

your children is that it strengthens the family bond and provides an opportunity to establish meaningful family rituals. Teens who attend religious services regularly—at least once a week—are at much lower risk of smoking, drinking, or using drugs than teens who never attend religious services. It is not likely that teenagers today will go to church, temple, or mosque on their own; it's usually something they do with their parents. Religious services and rituals like first communions, confirmations, and bar and bat mitzvahs also offer excellent opportunities for parental engagement and communication, and for instilling values in teens.

> If a family is positive, is healthy, if it's reinforcing, then
> the likelihood of its members getting into trouble with
> substances of abuse is diminished, and that's clearly a very
> strong emphasis of our [Mormon] faith.
>
> Glen R. Hanson, DDS, PhD, professor, University of
> Utah; director, Utah Addiction Center; former director
> of The National Institute on Drug Abuse (NIDA)

8. Get Dad Engaged—and Keep Him Engaged

Since parental engagement is a Mom-and-Pop operation, it's important that both Mom and Dad be engaged.

When Mom is engaged, children benefit. But when Mom and Dad are both engaged, their Parent Power is amplified: Fathers who are involved in their children's daily lives and keep open lines of communication with their children sharply reduce their children's risk of substance abuse.

Too often, Mom is the only engaged parent. In CASA's surveys, teens—both boys and girls—are more likely to report having an excellent relationship with their mother than with their father.

When we ask teens who have never smoked marijuana, "Why?" they tend to credit their decision to their mothers.

When we ask teens to whom they turn to discuss something very serious, they overwhelmingly answer, "Mom."

Children need their fathers to be there day after day, talking, listening, teaching, supporting, encouraging, and loving them. Mom needs Dad to be there too. If Dad is not engaged, Mom has no support in parenting—making decisions, setting rules, enforcing consequences, setting a good example. Children in two-parent families who report only poor or fair relationships with their fathers are at higher risk for substance abuse than those in single-parent families who have an excellent relationship with their mother or father.

Parents can divide some responsibilities of parental engagement. Perhaps Dad can't make it home for dinner but he can spend some time with the kids on the weekends. What is essential is that fathers as well as mothers lay a foundation of good communication with their children, that they talk and listen to them, set a good example with their own behavior, and that both fathers and mothers give the same, consistent messages about not smoking, drinking, or using drugs. Where Mom and Dad start from different views, it is important for them to come to a shared position before talking to their children.

There are many activities that can help get Dad engaged with the kids—dinner, playing sports or games like Scrabble, taking walks, coaching a team, helping with homework, collecting things together, even just driving the kids to and from their activities. Weekend (or longer) trips are a wonderful way for Dad to get involved. The YMCA Adventure Guides program organizes camping trips for fathers and their children. Any of these activities gives Dad a chance to show his interest in the child's hobbies, friends, school work, and development.

Of course, not every family has two parents. In twenty-first-century America, there are all kinds of families: those headed by Mom and Dad, Moms alone, Dads alone, Mom and Stepfather, Dad and Step-mother, grandmothers or grandfathers, aunts or uncles, even older siblings. Sometimes children have two families, with two sets of parents. What counts more than who heads the family, or how many heads the family has, is the engagement of those family heads—and the consistency of their messages about alcohol and drug use. An engaged single parent is more effective than disengaged fathers and mothers.

9. Engage with the Larger Community

Parental engagement should extend beyond the immediate family—to the larger family of a child's friends, schoolmates, teachers, neighbors, and the community. This larger family can serve as your support group and your child's safety net.

You may feel as though you are the only parent struggling to enforce rules or making difficult judgment calls, but the truth is that you are not alone and you don't need to do it alone. You are not the first parent ever to worry about how to keep your kids healthy and on the right track; I assure you there are other parents who have the same concerns.

Parents need support. Just as people have jogging buddies to help motivate them to get moving and keep moving, so too parents need parenting buddies. When your children are young, you have many

Concerned parents Thom and Deirdre Forbes created an online community chat group for local parents to share their concerns about what's going on with their kids. Parents can ask questions (even anonymously), share success stories and parenting tips (e.g., appropriate curfews), and discuss incidents that happen among teens in their community (arrests, house parties).

The Forbeses have found that the ideal parenting discussion group should be:

- Limited to parents of children in the same grade level
- Supplemented with periodic face-to-face meetings among the parents (every three months or so)
- Completely independent from the children's school

opportunities to get together with other parents—at school and community events, children's birthday parties, Mommy and Me class, PTA meetings—to talk about the challenges of being a parent. But as your children grow older, there may be fewer opportunities and you may feel more isolated.

As a fully engaged parent you should continue to develop meaningful relationships with the important people in your children's lives—the kinds of relationships that can make it easy to talk to parents in the community or the coach of your child's team about issues that concern you. Nurture your relationships with parents of your child's friends so that you don't have to face the challenges of raising a teenage son or daughter alone. Talk to other parents, ask what works and what doesn't work for them when they talk to their kids about risky behavior and substance use. If your child says you enforce the strictest curfew, check around. It's probably not true.

You can start a parent group in your own community through

your church or Little League team, or on the Internet by creating a Yahoo group or using a social networking website (Facebook, My-Space, Friendster) to get parents talking.

Developing close relationships with other families in your area can yield tangible benefits. Say you're concerned about what's going on at the parties your teenage son attends; you will have a much easier time calling the parents who are hosting those parties if you've met and talked with them. Indeed, in some communities the parents have come together voluntarily and signed pacts where they all agree not to host parties with alcohol or other drugs. With other parents on your side, you're not alone in making the difficult decisions about what to allow your own children to do. And your kids cannot tell you that your rules and standards are uniquely unjust; you can tell them with confidence that you happen to know their friends' parents are "just as horrible!"

Another benefit is that parents who have relationships with one another may be more inclined to step in when another's child is in trouble. Among mothers and fathers who have lost a child to a drug overdose or alcohol poisoning, there is a common, heart-wrenching refrain: "Our child's friends knew our child was using. Other parents at our child's school knew. Some of our neighbors knew. But no one said anything to us."

Engaged parents should accept responsibility to speak up when they learn that someone else's child is in trouble with drugs or alcohol, or when their own kids tell them a classmate or friend is using. In a sense, parents need to regard themselves as uncles and aunts—members of the larger family which is the community where they and their children live.

You and your children are likely to be part of another family—your religious community. Religious organizations can play a significant role in preventing and treating substance abuse in their communities. From offering substance-abuse prevention programs to parents

Wendy Gordon thinks it's time for the Jewish community to face the truth: Teenagers and adults are abusing alcohol and drugs. Gordon, a social worker, and member of Boca Raton Synagogue, is forming a team at the Orthodox congregation that will assist members with questions about addictions, with full confidentiality.

Lois Solomon, "Jewish Network to Help Fight Alcohol, Drug Abuse," *Sun-Sentinel*, April 7, 2008

and teens, to providing substance-abuse counseling, to including substance abuse as an issue in religious teachings, there are a variety of ways that religious organizations can reach out to folks in their community. If you are a member of a congregation or religious community, encourage your clergy and lay leaders to initiate programs to prevent substance abuse and learn where to refer individuals for treatment.

Your children spend most of their time with yet another family—their school. Parental engagement in your teen's school and that school's culture, policies, and practices is so critical that I have devoted Chapter 12, "How Can I Protect My Kids at School?" to this subject.

There are other larger families that can connect you to other members of your community and provide you with valuable resources.

One is the Partnership for a Drug-Free America, which is known for its antidrug TV commercials and newspaper ads. It has a website with interactive tools to provide parents with help in raising drug-free children. You can volunteer online at www.drugfree.org to join your local partnership affiliate.

The PTA—Parent Teacher Association—fosters parental involvement in families, schools, and communities to help children succeed.

Members are invited to come together to discuss issues, including raising drug-free kids, related to their children's growth and education. The PTA has local chapters in every state; to find yours, go to www.pta.org.

Another such family is made up of the 5,000 community antidrug coalitions in the U.S. supported by the Community Anti-Drug Coalitions of America (CADCA). A community coalition is a group of parents, teachers, law enforcement, businesses, religious leaders, health providers, and others who work locally to help make their communities drug-free. At www.cadca.org you can find an antidrug coalition in your community.

THE IMPORTANCE OF BEING A PARENT

Above all, remember these words: *Parents are not pals.*

In all your discussions and decisions, be careful not to cross the line from parenthood to friendship. Your job is not to be your child's friend, but to be your child's teacher, and source of parental love and

---

The students made a persuasive plea for parents who set clear boundaries. What really set them off was the bad behavior of mothers and fathers who drink with kids, who supply alcohol, who seem oblivious to their children's problems. "I have less respect for those parents," said one boy. "They think they're the cool parents. But they're not responsible." What some parents don't get, several kids said, is that "nobody cares if the parents are cool." What they do crave is parents who act like parents.

Marc Fisher, "Are You a Toxic Parent?"
Washington Post Magazine, July 30, 2006

---

discipline, to establish standards of conduct and to provide your child with a moral compass. Your children will not thank you for being a pal; at some point, they may wonder whether you care enough about them to be a parent.

Your kid will make plenty of friends over a lifetime, but the number of parents your son or daughter has been allotted is limited. If you fail to assume this role in your son or daughter's life, where will they turn when what they really want—and need—is not another pal, but a parent?

2

TALK TO YOUR KIDS ABOUT SMOKING, DRINKING, AND DRUGS

Communication—talking, listening, and guiding—is the core of parental engagement. You need to be able to talk with your children about difficult issues, including substance abuse, to get them to talk to you honestly about what's going on in their lives, and to guide them to make healthy, sensible decisions.

But how?

With a teenager especially, how do you connect on a level that is comfortable and natural?

How do you become engaged in your son's life without making him feel as if you are invading his space? How do you ask questions without making your daughter feel like she's being interrogated?

How do you talk about substance use (or other risky behaviors) without it turning into a confrontation or a fight? Without getting a "You don't trust me!" shouted back?

The first step in building good communication is to start early spending quality time just talking to your child—in the car, during dinner, watching TV, going to church, at ball games, walking the dog, playing games, in the park, on vacation—using the moments you have together to get to know your kids and to let your kids get to know you. Talk about anything and everything, it doesn't matter so much what the subject is as long as you and your children are communicating openly. Your children won't feel comfortable talking about difficult issues, like drugs and alcohol, if they don't feel that it's normal to talk to you about what's going on in their lives.

With a solid foundation of open, two-way communication, cemented by talking and listening to your child, you will have the Parent Power to guide your child to make the right decisions if your guidance has the ring of authenticity to both of you.

What do I mean by authenticity? Your guidance to your child on making healthy, drug-free decisions and the discussion that accompanies it will have authenticity if they are based on facts and nourished by love.

Speaking truth in love, we may grow up in all things . . .

Ephesians 4:15

KNOW THE FACTS AND
STICK TO THE FACTS

The facts I set out in Chapters 4 and 5 give you plenty of accurate information to help you make the case that your teen should stay away from drugs. Use that information confidently. You have science and medicine and the law on your side. You don't need to exaggerate or embellish the dangers of tobacco, alcohol, and drug use. If you exaggerate those dangers, your kids will smell a rat.

Be realistic about why people abuse alcohol and other drugs.

For example, they can make you feel good and forget about your problems—but only temporarily. Underscore that while it may seem to your child that marijuana and other illegal drugs are everywhere, most people don't use them and haven't tried them.

If you can't answer all your child's questions or you don't know all the facts about a drug your son or daughter asks about, just admit it. If you're not sure of something, tell them that and say, "Let's find out together." For instance: "I'm not sure exactly what meth does to your body, but I've seen the ads on TV and they worry me. What do you think it does? Let's learn more about this together." You and your child can start by reading the "Parent Power Glossary for Parents and Teens" in this book; you can also consult other resources from the library, visit health or government websites like www.nida.nih.gov, or ask your doctor for more information.

Take advantage of opportunities in the news to talk to your teen. When there's a story on television or in the papers about a drug overdose, celebrity antics under the influence of alcohol or drugs, or a drunk-driving incident, use it to open up a conversation and probe your teen's reaction.

When you talk to your kids, focus on facts that are relevant to them. Let's say you're talking about why smoking is bad. Describing the long term dangers of smoking—lung cancer, heart disease, chronic bronchitis, and emphysema—will make their eyes glaze over. Most teens have a sense of invulnerability, that they are immortal, impervious to harm; for them, those are diseases that happen to "old people."

If you see an ad for cigarettes with your child, point out that the tobacco companies are trying to manipulate kids to get them addicted to their product so that the companies can profit from their habit. Say, "Don't let the tobacco companies make a sucker out of you." If your child tells you that friends or classmates smoke, say, "The cigarettes smoke, your friends are just the suckers on the other end."

Use pithy examples. Telling your teenage children that "Kissing a smoker is like licking a dirty ashtray" might make the point be-

The important thing is to have the facts and say the correct thing. Don't scare them. Scaring doesn't work; lying doesn't work. Honest information works.

Cynthia Kuhn, PhD, professor of pharmacology,
Duke University Medical Center, at CASA's
Family Matters Conference, 2004

cause they're likely to hear it from, or tell it to, their boyfriend or girlfriend.

COMMUNICATION STARTS WITH YOU

Let's say you want to have a conversation with your son about drugs in school. Imagine you begin by lecturing him about not using drugs. Your son listens in silence.

You say, "Are you listening to me?"

Your son says, "Yes," and then goes to his room and shuts the door.

That wasn't much of a conversation, was it?

If you want to be able to talk about substance abuse (or any difficult issue) in a comfortable way with your child, you need to establish the lines of communication well beforehand, by encouraging conversations when your child is younger. Conversations are also a give-and-take operation: Make sure that you are receiving (listening) as much as you are giving (talking). Sometimes an open mind and an open ear are the best things you can bring to a conversation with your teenager.

Here is an example of how a productive conversation with your child might sound:

Parent: "Why do you think someone your age would want to smoke marijuana?"

Teen: "I dunno. To be cool, probably. Maybe just to try it."

Parent: "Do you think that smoking pot is a cool idea for someone your age?"

Teen: "Well, probably you would get into trouble if you got caught, so that's dumb. But I dunno. Lots of older kids do it."

Parent: "Did you know that marijuana is addictive? It affects your ability to think and to learn. Also smoking pot when you're young increases your risk of getting hooked on other drugs."

Teen: "Really? I didn't know all that! Well then how come everyone does it?"

Parent: "Actually, everyone doesn't do it. Most kids don't smoke marijuana. In any case, your [father/mother] and I know that you're smart and you'll make healthy choices about what you put into your body."

You need to get to the point where spending time alone talking to your child feels natural to both of you. The goal is to really get to know your child—your child's hopes, fears, likes, and dislikes—and to have your child get to know you too! Your child will be comfortable discussing difficult issues with you if he knows what your views are, what your parenting style is, and that you'll react to the difficult truths your child may reveal without yelling and/or rushing to conclusions. Self-discipline on your part is important. Balancing understanding and firm guidance is no easy task, but if you master it, you will find your child more willing to talk to you about the problems

When your kids say, "You don't understand what's going on," you need to say, "You're right, I don't. What I gather is that my experience was quite different from yours, that you are experiencing pressures that I never did. So what I need is for you to help me understand what you're going through by explaining it to me."

Dr. Ralph Lopez, pediatrician and author

Dealing with Excuses

Adolescents are "the experts" on why it's okay to use certain substances: "Marijuana is a natural herb." Avoid getting into such debates; they will derail you. The adolescent is rationalizing why her actions are okay, and won't listen to your logical responses or appreciate your point of view. The child may be feeling unheard, invalidated, or judged, causing her to interpret your words as condemning. The fact that you are concerned and care deeply about her may become lost in such debates.

Instead, you might try responding, "Well, maybe you're right, marijuana is a plant. . . ." This validates your child's perspective and demonstrates that you're willing to really listen. Then you can begin a dialogue about why substance abuse is interesting or important to your child. Once your child feels that you are willing to listen, she may be more open to considering your position: "Is smoking pot really the best choice for you? What do you think are the benefits and risks of taking drugs? How will drugs affect you in achieving your future goals?"

James Rao, LMSW, social worker, Mount Sinai Adolescent Health Center

he faces. Once you and your child are comfortable talking to one another, you can persuasively convey important messages about what behavior is—and is not—acceptable for your family.

Year after year, when CASA surveys ask teens what issues are their greatest concern, teens name drugs more than any other. Social pressures are close behind, and social pressures probably include the pressure to do drugs. These concerns are well ahead of getting good grades, getting into college, sexual pressures, crime and violence, being bullied, or getting a job. Your kids are concerned about drugs, and they want to talk to you about their concerns. But your children may hesitate, or feel uncomfortable discussing their concerns, or even refuse to talk to you if you haven't established ongoing communication with them or if they believe you will be hostile in response to their honesty.

The better you are at listening, the likelier your child is to open up to you and to listen to you. Parents who are not good listeners should not be surprised if their children don't pay attention to them. If you want your children to listen to you and respect your opinions, give your kids lots of opportunities to talk to you about the things that matter to them.

Being a good listener takes some practice. Give your children your undivided attention. Make eye contact. Paraphrase what they've said to confirm that you've heard them correctly. Ask open-ended follow-up questions to encourage conversation. Don't interrupt or jump too quickly to fill in silences; allow your children to express themselves fully.

WHAT IF YOUR CHILD TELLS YOU THAT A FRIEND IS DOING DRUGS?

It's not easy for your teens to tell you that one of their best friends (whom they know you know) or a kid at their school smokes pot. Or that they are dating someone who gets drunk on the weekends. Or that a classmate sells marijuana or pills like Adderall in school. Only if you have been broadly engaged and have established a history of listening to your child is your son or daughter likely to open up to you on such subjects.

Teens who confide to their parents about a friend's drug use may plead with their parents not to "snitch" on their friend. Before confiding, they may ask you to promise not to tell their friend's parents. You may fear that if you talk to that friend's parents, your teen will never again confide in you. If your child is hesitant about letting you call the friend's parents, explain that a good friend would risk their friend's anger to save the friend.

If your child tells you about a friend's drug use, ask yourself why your child is telling you. Is your child looking for a reaction, curious to see if you become alarmed or think that it's "no big deal"? Is your child probing to see how you'd react if he were using drugs? Is your child trying to figure out what he should do about his friend? Does your child genuinely want your help in getting help for the friend?

If you discover that a child in your community is drinking or

---

Q: If your child told you that a friend was drinking or using drugs, would you call that friend's parents and tell them?

A: I use discretion. Once, I told a mother something I knew to be true about her daughter's use of alcohol. She told her daughter I had called, the daughter denied the accusation, and that was the end of it . . . for them. Unfortunately, it drove a wedge between me and my daughter that took years to heal; wasn't worth it. That said, I have also told parents who were grateful for the information and who kept the source of the information confidential. My inclination is to tell, but I am careful.

A: I would immediately notify parents! We're also aware that our children and some parents wouldn't accept our intervention gracefully. Some families would leap into action and some would continue in denial to the detriment of the family.

Parent postings on CASA Parent Power discussion forum

---

using drugs, the best way to help that child is to contact the child's parents directly. Calling won't be easy. None of us wants to be the bearer of bad news, especially about someone else's child. Parents who hear that their child is drinking or using drugs may not be receptive to such news. Their denial or disbelief is part of a devastating culture of silence about teen substance abuse, fueled by stigma and parental embarrassment. So be prepared to receive an unwelcoming reaction from the parents, but rest assured that you are doing them and their child a favor.

Parents also need to nourish a sense of responsibility in their own teens to watch out for one another, to explain that an essential part of friendship is getting help for their friends who are using, not covering up their drug or alcohol use. Children should be encouraged to speak up when they have a friend or classmate who is dealing or using. The point is not to punish the user, but to help assure that children (and families) who need help get it—and the sooner the better, because the earlier help is provided, the greater the chance of success.

Parents should also encourage their children to seek medical help immediately when a friend is in trouble. Too often, teens abandon a

One day, I was upstairs in my bedroom and I could hear a phone conversation through the central heating duct—it was my son, Danny. Danny was organizing a marijuana buy for himself and his friends. There were about twelve kids involved, all from the "best" families in our neighborhood. I called their parents and requested that we meet to discuss the issues of drugs and alcohol. Over the phone, several parents were indignant. Of the twelve families, parents from only three showed up—my wife and I and two other parents, each without their respective spouses.

—Daniel P. Reardon, DDS

Irma was a fourteen-year-old girl from Belmont, California, who took an ecstasy pill on April 23, 2004. She became sick immediately—vomiting and writhing in pain—yet her friends did not seek medical help for her. Instead, they gave her marijuana, thinking it would relax her and possibly help her because they had heard it had medicinal qualities. Irma suffered for hours and when she was finally taken to the hospital the next morning, she was in terrible shape. Five days later she was taken off life support and died.

Drug Enforcement Agency (DEA) website, *Just Think Twice*

friend who needs medical attention because of a drug or alcohol overdose. Children who are afraid of getting "busted" or getting into trouble may be too scared to call for help. Or they may not call because they aren't aware of how serious the danger is. Teach your children that when a friend is in medical trouble, they should always call 911; the call can be made anonymously and it can save their friend's life.

IF YOUR CHILD ASKS, "DID YOU DO DRUGS?", IT'S TIME TO TALK

What do you do if your child asks you, point blank, "Mom [or Dad], did you smoke marijuana when you were a kid?" Whether your answer is yes or no, the ensuing discussion shouldn't be about you, but about your child and why he's asking, and how your child's choices about substance use will affect his future. Your child has just opened the window for you to start a conversation about substance use, so take advantage of the opportunity!

If your child is asking you this question, it's probably because something happened and your child is wondering what behavior is right for him or her. So before you disclose anything, find out *why* your child is asking the question. "What makes you ask, honey? Did you see or hear something that made you wonder if I ever smoked pot?" Maybe a friend's parents smoke pot in front of their kids, and your child wants to know if that's "normal." Or maybe a friend offered your child a joint and said, "Everyone smokes pot when they're young." By finding out what information your child really wants to know, you can direct your response appropriately.

Diverting the conversation back to your child—"Let's talk about you"—is a useful psychological tool and you have every right to use it. After all, it's one of the perks of being the parent. And you don't want to miss this key opportunity to guide your child to make healthy, drug-free choices.

USE YOUR PERSONAL EXPERIENCES AS A TEACHING TOOL

There's no consensus, no hard-and-fast rule, about how you should answer your child's question about your own history of alcohol and drug use. Whether and what to tell your child will vary from family to family, depending on the situation of the child (age, risk factors, etc.) and the experience of the parents.

If you didn't drink, smoke tobacco, or use marijuana or other drugs, the answer may seem obvious: "No." But when you tell your child that you never tried it, be prepared for the possibility that your child will say, "Then how can you say it's dangerous or bad for me?" You can point out that there are lots of things we've never tried that we know are bad for us. There are many examples you can use. Perhaps you have a story about a friend who got into trouble as a result of drinking or drug use. Or you can rely on your own good judgment. "You don't have to put your hand into a flame to tell your little boy or girl not to do it."

How and what you tell your children about your own substance use is critical. If you did use drugs when you were a teen or in college, do not lie about it. If you lie, you can lose credibility with your children and that is a sure way of eroding your Parent Power. That doesn't mean you have to tell your kids everything about your drug use, any more than you would tell them about your sex life or personal or family finances. But whatever you do share with your children, be sure to emphasize that you don't want your children to make the same mistake and explain why. You can tell them, "We know a lot more today about the dangers of drug use than we did when I was growing up."

Telling the truth doesn't mean disclosing everything. Remember, you are the parent; your job is to keep your kids safe and healthy. As the authority figure, you have the right to tell your child only what you think is appropriate for a parent to disclose. There's no parental obligation to disclose your childhood foibles.

Your negative experiences are important teaching points to share with your children. Say you were at a party in high school or college and everyone started smoking pot but you didn't want to, so you went home. This story illustrates that you had the wisdom and courage to withstand peer pressure, and can inspire your children to do the same. If you or a friend or a classmate got into serious trouble because of drinking or drugs—became addicted, had a car accident, were sexually assaulted—you should use those stories to illustrate the dangers

---

Suppose your kid asks you, "Why should I tell you about what I'm doing if you won't tell me?"

You can respond, "Because we're not friends. This isn't an equal relationship. I'm the parent. My job is to make sure that you grow up. Your job is to grow up."

Dr. Ralph Lopez, pediatrician and author

of substance abuse, and to reinforce your message that your children shouldn't repeat your mistakes or those of your friends.

If you decide to tell your children about your own history of drug use or underage drinking, make it clear that in retrospect it was a big mistake. Focus on the fact that we know a lot more now about how harmful smoking, drinking, and drugs (especially marijuana) can be for teens. Also describe any negative aspects of your experience. This can assure that your children don't take your past conduct as proof that such behavior is a normal part of growing up or as a signal that you won't punish them for doing the same things you did. Here are some examples:

"Yes, I smoked pot and it was a big mistake. It made me paranoid and stupid and I got into trouble with my parents."

"Back then, we didn't know how bad cigarettes and marijuana are for you. When I was your age, many of us smoked cigarettes. We thought it was sophisticated, like the movie stars. We didn't know what we know today about the cancers, heart attacks, and emphysema that cigarettes cause. So it is with marijuana. We know a lot more about marijuana today than we did years ago, and it's a more immedi-

---

Q: If you smoked marijuana, abused alcohol, or used illegal drugs at any point in your life, did you tell your kids about it? What did you say?

A: I told my kids that I experimented with pot and used way more alcohol than I should have. I always included the bad effects it caused, whether it was bad effects with my friendships, dates, driving, etc., to show that it was not okay. Be honest about your use, but always talk about the negative aspects of your use. Kids appreciate honesty.

Parent posting on CASA Parent Power discussion forum

ate threat to you than cigarettes were when I was a teenager. Marijuana today is much stronger than it was when I was in college. We now know that it's addictive and can damage your developing brain and affect your memory, ability to concentrate, and learning skills."

"I had a friend who talked me into trying cocaine. I did it once and didn't really like it, but my friend got addicted to it and had to drop out of college to get treatment. It was a dumb risk to take and I'm just plain lucky that I didn't get hooked. My parents didn't talk to me about drugs so I didn't know better. I want you to be educated so that you can make smarter decisions than I did."

PARENT TIPS

- Early on, establish an open dialogue with your children and make your expectations about their substance use clear.
- Make talking with your children about substance use a natural part of your continuing discussion with them, rather than just a one-time event.
- When discussing alcohol and other drugs, be honest and focus on the facts appropriate to your child's developmental stage.
- Use news events, TV shows, or real life occurrences as teaching opportunities.
- If your child asks about your history of substance use, don't lie, but focus your response on your child and why your child is asking.
- Teach your child that being a good friend means getting help for a friend who abuses substances.

3

EAT MEALS TOGETHER— DINNER MAKES A DIFFERENCE

How do you get to know your children—what makes them tick, what concerns them, what's going on in their daily lives, at school, and with their friends? How do you get to know when something's wrong?

By being with them daily . . . and there's no more comfortable or natural way to do that than having dinner together each night. That's the ideal, but if you can't have dinner together each night, I have some other suggestions for you at the end of this chapter.

FREQUENT FAMILY DINNERS PREVENT SUBSTANCE USE

In the 1996 CASA survey of teens, I noticed that kids who had dinner with their parents every night of the week were far less likely to smoke, drink, or use drugs than kids who never had dinner with their parents. The kids who had frequent family dinners also tended to get A's and B's in school, were less likely to be stressed out, perpetually bored, or have friends who smoked, drank, or used drugs.

So we started calibrating our surveys and research and discovered this: As the number of days a week that parents have dinner with their children goes up, the risk that those children will get involved with tobacco, alcohol, or drugs goes down! Simply put, the more often children eat dinner with their parents, the less likely they are to smoke, drink, or use drugs. That's why I consider family dinner a most comfortable and powerful tool you can use to keep kids off drugs.

This phenomenon has less to do with the food that's on the plates and more to do with what's happening at the table. The nightly ritual of a family dinner gives families a relaxed, nourishing context for coming together, connecting and communicating, talking and listening, seeing and hearing. It's where parental engagement happens. Insisting that your tweens and teens be at the family dinner table each night is an exercise of Parent Power at its best.

Parents who dine with their children every night know where their kids are in the evening, whether homework has been done. They can get a sense of what's on their kids' minds, who their kids' friends are, what their kids are interested in, and how their moods change.

The nightly family dinner gives parents an opportunity to talk to

---

Bette Midler and her daughter Sophie appeared as guests on *The Oprah Winfrey Show*, June 18, 2008. Oprah asked Bette what she thought was the best thing she had done, as a parent.

Bette Midler responded, "I think the best thing that my husband and I did was we had dinner with her every single night of her life."

their children on a regular basis. And it sends your kids these important messages:

I am here for you every night of the week.

Need to talk about something? I'm here.

Want to ask me something? I'm here.

Want to boast or complain about something? I'm here.

And it will help keep your kids honest and accountable if they know you'll be seeing them every night.

THE DIFFERENCE DINNER MAKES

Why is the family dinner so important in raising drug-free kids? Because it shows how much you care about your children, and this knowledge affects all aspects of their life.

Kids appreciate it when Mom and Dad make a point of being there at dinner most every night. With both parents working, or Dad or Mom holding down two jobs to make ends meet, children realize that your being there shows a deep level of engagement. Being there for dinner creates big benefits for your children's mental, physical, and academic well-being. Here are some of them:

- You'll stay up to speed on how your children are doing in school and be able to intervene if there's a problem. If your kids are struggling with a particular subject, you'll hear about it and be able to help. If they're slacking off, skipping school, not handing in assignments, you'll be able to figure out why and try to change their behavior. If they have a learning disability, you'll pick it up faster and be able to deal with it.

- You'll be able to see how your children are doing emotionally. Are they depressed, anxious, stressed out, or perpetually bored? It's important that you pick up on these things because they are all risk factors for smoking, drinking, and using drugs. You can help your children overcome these feelings if you know what's going on.

- Your children's friends can influence your child's behavior and views on substance use. Teens who have dinner with their families at least five times a week are less likely to have friends who drink and smoke pot or to go to parties where alcohol and drugs are available.

- Having dinner every day means that it's much harder to hide smoking, drinking, or drugging from Mom and Dad. Children who think that their parents won't catch them or won't enforce any consequences if they smoke, drink, or get high are more likely to do so.

- Teens who have dinner with their families at least five times a week are less likely to say that they can buy marijuana within a day. The faster kids can get their hands on the drug, the greater the chances that they're using it.

HOW TO GET CHILDREN TALKING
AT THE DINNER TABLE

Parents of teenagers, especially older teens, often think that their kids don't want to sit around the dinner table and talk to them. But at CASA we've talked to hundreds of teens. We've surveyed thousands

---

Why do family dinners work? Studies suggest that frequent family dinners foster closer family ties, may be helpful in teaching children coping skills, enhance family communication, and provide good role modeling.

Franko, et al. "What Mediates the Relationship Between Family Meals and Adolescent Health Issues?" *Health Psychology*, vol. 27 (March 2008)

---

more. Kids do in fact crave the family dinner and the connecting that comes with it. We asked teens whether they prefer to have dinner with their families or eat alone, and more than eight out of ten teens of all ages preferred to have dinner with their families. And what they want at dinner is to talk to you.

Back in the 1950s, there was a book about childhood and parenting titled: *"Where did you go?" "Out." "What did you do?" "Nothing."*

That's an exchange typical in families where there is little or no communication between parents and teenagers. Parents who sit at the dinner table with their kids day in and day out can learn to turn such exchanges into more robust conversations. The key is to make talking about anything and everything part of your normal family routine, and establishing that free exchange as early in life as possible.

CONVERSATION STARTERS

One great way to get your kids talking at dinner is to use conversation starters.

When children are young, appropriate conversation starters might be questions about their world:

- What's the best and worst thing that happened today?
- What's your favorite place in the house to hang out?
- If you were in charge of the music for our family vacation, which songs would you pick?
- Which TV family is the most fun to watch?
- What do you like about your friends?
- What's your favorite amusement park? What's your favorite ride?
- What's your favorite smell?
- If you could have a wild animal from anywhere in the world as a pet, what animal would you choose?
- What's the greatest invention of all time?

When I became concerned that my teenage son might be getting involved with the wrong kids and with alcohol and drugs, I wasn't sure what to do. As an immediate first step, I started requiring that he be home five nights a week for dinner. Over the next several months, I noticed a dramatic positive change in my son. I know family dinners have a positive influence on children because I watched my son change and saw improvements in his behavior, school performance, and social interaction.

Steve Burd, president and CEO of US supermarket chain Safeway

- Using one word, how would you describe your family?
- What do you want to be when you grow up?
- What do you most like to do with the family?

Dinner conversations are the perfect opportunity to instill values in your children when they enter the later tween and teen years. Appropriate topics for conversations at this stage would include current events, family matters, topics of special interest to your family (film, sports, philosophy, politics, religion), goals, difficult situations, and such questions as:

- What's the best and worst thing that happened today?
- What values are most important to you?
- Who's the greatest athlete of all time?
- What can we each do to make the world a better place? What can we do as a family?
- What can we, as a family, do to improve our communication?
- Who's your favorite teacher (coach, role model) and why?
- What's your favorite subject in school?

- What would you do if your best friend started using marijuana (OxyContin, cocaine)?
- What three things do you want to accomplish this year?
- What do you want to be when you grow up?
- What's your favorite movie? Band/musician? Sports team?
- What do you think of last week's sermon?

At CASA, we consider the family dinner so important that we have created a national day of celebration, "CASA Family Day—A Day to Eat Dinner with Your Children™." Family Day is celebrated every year on the fourth Monday in September, as a reminder to parents of the importance of family dinners. The president, the governors of all the states, and hundreds of cities and counties recognize the importance of family dinners by proclaiming Family Day every year. Lots of community organizations, churches, schools, and social centers celebrate Family Day. For more information about Family Day, and for ideas about how to make dinner together fun, visit our website at www.CASAFamilyDay.org.

If you make every day Family Day, you will take a giant step toward raising your children to be emotionally and physically healthy, academically successful, and drug and alcohol free.

Kids know how much effort it takes to be a good parent. They know when you care enough to create a structured family life that provides a regular, ritualized forum for closeness and intimacy—the family dinner, the shared vacation, participation in their interests and activities.

Dan Kindlon, *Too Much of a Good Thing* (2003)

WHAT IF I CAN'T MAKE IT TO DINNER?

What if you work at night? Or can't get home in time for dinner? Or your teen has so many activities, there's no time to sit down for dinner as a family? These are all questions I've been asked by caring parents.

Although having dinner is the easiest way to create routine opportunities for engagement and communication, you can certainly find other ways to spend time together that fit into your family's schedule. If your schedule can't be rearranged, engage in other kinds of activities with your kids, so that you are a reliable, involved, and interested presence in their lives. Remember, it's not the food that's working the

Family Meetings

Family bonding helps to prevent adolescent health and behavior problems, including substance abuse. Parents can strengthen family bonds by providing children with opportunities for involvement in the family.

One way to do this is by conducting regular family meetings. Family meetings provide family members with a sense of belonging and an opportunity to discuss important issues or share concerns. To break the ice and reinforce the idea that family meetings are not a "bore," the agenda for the first meeting should be planning a fun family activity. Everyone can make a suggestion and then the family can chose one activity and plan it. In subsequent meetings, you can develop a family contract about alcohol and other drug use. (See Chapter 8, "How Can I Make My Home a Safe Haven?" for more information about family contracts.)

From *Guiding Good Choices*®, a family competency training program

magic at those dinners—it's you. Creating opportunities to connect is what's key.

Here are some suggestions for other ways to create regular family time with your children:

- Share every available meal on the weekends.
- Have breakfast together.
- Take your child out to lunch once a week or once in a while.
- Go for walks together after work/school or on the weekends.
- Take advantage of one-on-one time in the car—offer to drive your kids to or from school, to their activities, friends' houses, movies.
- Take miniholidays together, like afternoon trips to visit family, or go to museums, parks, or other towns.
- Have family meetings.
- Don't overschedule your child's after-school activities.

Your kids need to know you are there for them. So make yourself available. Enjoy your time together. And remember, what your kids want most, at dinner or during the time you spend together, is you.

PART II

RECOGNIZE IT

4

WHAT DRUGS ARE LIKELIEST TO TEMPT YOUR TEEN?

The substances your teen is sure to be offered and most likely to try are cigarettes, alcohol (beer and sweetened distilled spirits), marijuana, and prescription drugs.

Why these substances?

Because they are widely available and relatively inexpensive. In the case of cigarettes and alcohol, large corporations, like those that own Marlboro, Newport, Budweiser and Miller beer and produce distilled spirits like vodka, make big bucks when your teen buys their products—despite the fact that it is both illegal and harmful for teens to do so.

These tempting teen drugs all share addictive characteristics. Abuse of them is associated with negative psychological, physical, neurological, and social consequences. Alcohol and prescription drugs can seriously harm your child, and can be fatal when taken in excess or mixed together. Yet many kids do just that.

Marijuana is illegal. If that's not a convincing enough reason to forbid your children from using it, I'll provide you with detailed information about how marijuana negatively affects children's coordination, memory, and learning, and can affect their neurological and emotional development.

There are many different drugs that your teenager might be offered or try—designer drugs like ecstasy and GHB (the date rape drug); street drugs like cocaine, heroin, and meth; and new drugs like salvia, an herbal hallucinogen. The "Parent Power Glossary for Parents and Teens" will give you a general understanding of all these drugs. But by and large teen drug abuse involves tobacco, alcohol, marijuana, and prescription drugs. In this chapter, you'll learn more about these drugs so you will be equipped to steer your children away from them. And you'll also learn about steroids, which your teen athletes may be offered.

TOBACCO: THE NUMBER ONE KILLER

You're undoubtedly aware of the deadly and crippling heart disease, cancer, and respiratory ailments caused by smoking. You know that tobacco use during adolescence can set kids on a path of lifelong addiction, chronic illness, and premature death. I won't repeat all those frightening facts here. What I do want to tell you is how you can keep your children from smoking.

Why is this so important? Because there is now evidence that nicotine may make the young brain more susceptible to other drugs like alcohol or marijuana. Because if your kids resist cigarettes while they're still young, the chance that they will go on to become adult smokers is slim to none. And because about one out of three adolescents who try smoking will end up addicted to nicotine as adults.

Virtually all adult smokers got hooked on cigarettes before they reached age twenty-one, most while teens and preteens. Teens are likely to experience the stress-relieving effects of nicotine more strongly than adults. Teens who smoke develop a more deeply ingrained reward pattern than adults, which leads to addiction.

The tobacco companies have known this for decades. That's why they are relentless in trying to get your child to light up, chew tobacco, or try snuff. In 2004, faced with declining sales, R.J. Reynolds began marketing candy-flavored cigarettes in order to disguise the harsh taste of tobacco and entice youngsters to smoke. Public outcry forced the company to withdraw these products from the market. But Big Tobacco will keep trying to find ways to make smoking more attractive to children, which is why you should be vigilant in helping your child resist trying this addictive, crippling product.

The key to preventing cigarette addiction is to understand why your child will be tempted to smoke. Advertising, movies, TV shows, and other media messages often lead children to think that smoking is cool. Many kids see smoking as a way to appear grown-up or sophisticated. In Chapter 11, "How Can I Mitigate the Media's Influence?",

I'll give you pointers on how to teach your children to decode and resist advertising and other media messages designed to make smoking attractive.

Teens who start smoking at an early age, say twelve to fourteen, and teens who smoke regularly, are more likely than their nonsmoking peers to suffer from depression, anxiety, or low self-esteem. If your teen starts smoking at a young age or is a regular smoker, try to find out if she is struggling with such problems. If so, seek professional advice because it may be essential to deal with the underlying problem before you can convince your child to quit smoking.

The good news is that society is on your side in this battle. There has been a seismic cultural shift away from smoking over the past thirty years, since as U.S. secretary of Health, Education, and Welfare, I mounted the nation's first antismoking campaign in 1978. Public health education campaigns, coupled with increased taxes, bans on smoking in public places, and other initiatives have reduced smoking in this country. Once marketed as the paradigm of cool, smoking has become, in many circles, particularly among the more educated and affluent, socially unacceptable. Unfortunately, smokeless tobacco use among teen boys is on the rise, so make sure your children know that dip, chew, and snuff are dangerous too.

ALCOHOL: THE MOST POPULAR TEEN DRUG

It may be illegal for your teen to buy beer, wine, sweetened distilled spirits such as alcopops, and liquor like vodka, but that hasn't stopped the alcohol industry from profiting from underage drinking. In 2001, underage drinking accounted for 18 percent of alcohol industry sales. That's some twenty-three billion dollars, and you can bet that the alcohol industry is doing its best to keep making those bucks, year after year, by enticing your children to drink.

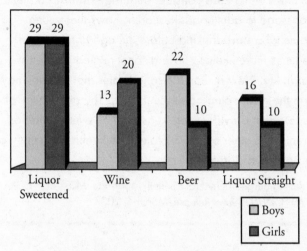

Alcoholic Beverage Preferences of Teen Boys and Girls by Percentage

CASA. National Survey of American Attitudes on Substance Abuse XIII: Teens and Parents (2008)

The preferred alcoholic beverages among underage boys and girls are sweetened liquor drinks, followed by beer for boys and wine for girls. As you will learn in Chapter 11, your children are exposed to extensive promotion of these products, which in turn increases their desire to drink them. For example, beer is sold and advertised heavily in sporting arenas and at concerts, where teenagers congregate. In Chapter 11 I'll explain these marketing strategies and how you can reduce your child's exposure to them and their influence on your child.

Beer and sweetened alcohol appeal to the palates and pocketbooks of young drinkers. These drinks are much cheaper than spirits and wine. Because beer and alcopops are sold in corner stores (where drinking age laws tend to be less diligently enforced) and supermarkets, they are often easier to purchase without a valid ID. Beer is also a large part of high school and college iconography—keg parties, beer pong, T-shirts with beer slogans, movies like *Animal House* and *Strange Brew*, and MTV's *Spring Break* broadcasts.

Too many Americans consider underage drinking a rite of passage to adulthood. Research shows that young people who start drinking before the age of fifteen are five times more likely to have alcohol-related problems later in life. New research also indicates that alcohol may harm the developing adolescent brain. The availability of this research provides more reasons than ever before for parents and other adults to protect the health and safety of our nation's children.

Acting Surgeon General Kenneth Moritsugu, MD, MPH, *DHHS News Release,* March 6, 2007

One reason that underage drinking is so common is that alcohol is available in so many homes. Another reason is that teens, and many adults, tend to view drinking alcohol as a normal and socially acceptable activity. Alcohol is at the heart of many cherished occasions and religious traditions. Your children are likely to see you or other family members drinking at home, at celebrations, or as part of a religious ceremony. Moderate adult drinking is widely accepted.

Understanding what drinking means for children and teens, and the scientific rationale for delaying drinking until age twenty-one, will help you convey to your children a credible, meaningful argument against teen drinking.

Research shows that, like other drugs, alcohol negatively impacts adolescent brain development. As Dr. Aaron White of Duke Medical Center, one of the nation's experts on the effects of drug use on the adolescent brain, explains, "There are long-term cognitive consequences to excessive drinking of alcohol in adolescence." Teens who drink heavily savage their memory, attention span, and spatial skills. Alcohol-dependent youth fare worse on language and memory tests.

The developing brain of an adolescent is a precious, complex, sensitive device that is more vulnerable to the damaging and addictive effects of alcohol. Daily or excessive alcohol use during this time of critical brain development can cause permanent changes in the way your child's brain works. The more frequently teens drink, the more likely they are to destroy significantly greater mental capacity than older drinkers. Dr. White considers recent discoveries about the damage caused to the teen brain by heavy drinking to be as important as the scientific discovery of "what a bad thing it was for pregnant women to drink."

Studies have shown that the hippocampus, a part of the brain that develops during adolescence and is key to memory and learning, is smaller in adults who drank heavily during their teenage years. That's because introducing lots of alcohol to the brain during those years disrupts brain development and can lead to permanently reduced brain function.

If your teen is drinking, it is likely in excess, often with the intent to get drunk. Teens are less likely than adults to drink moderately. Roughly 20 percent of seventeen-year-olds engage in binge drinking in any given month, 5 percent of them on more than a few occasions.

Beyond their penchant for taking risks and seeking thrills, scientific evidence suggests that teen drinkers are less sensitive to the sedative and dis-coordinating consequences of drinking alcohol: Teens

---

Adolescents drink less frequently than adults, but when they do drink, they drink more heavily than adults. When youth between the ages of twelve and twenty consume alcohol, they drink on average about five drinks per occasion about six times a month.

The Surgeon General's Call to Action to Prevent and Reduce Underage Drinking, 2007

Alcohol use by young people is dangerous, not only because of the risks associated with acute impairment, but also because of the threat to their long-term development and well-being. Traffic crashes are perhaps the most visible of these dangers, with alcohol being implicated in nearly one-third of youth traffic fatalities. Underage alcohol use is also associated with violence, suicide, educational failure, and other problem behaviors. All of these problems are magnified by early onset of teen drinking: the younger the drinker, the worse the problem.

National Research Council and National Academy of Sciences Institute of Medicine, *Reducing Underage Drinking: A Collective Responsibility,* 2004

don't become sleepy as easily or lose their balance as quickly. Teens can physically drink more, and longer, than adults, which opens the way to dangerous binge-drinking behavior.

There are immediate consequences to teen alcohol abuse: unintended, unprotected sex with several partners, poor grades, auto accidents, fighting, and rape. Alcohol is implicated in the top three causes of teen deaths: accidents (including traffic fatalities and drowning), homicide, and suicide. The National Highway Traffic Safety Administration estimates that raising the minimum drinking age from eighteen to twenty-one has saved the lives of nine hundred teens on the road each year.

The younger your child starts to drink, the more likely he is to have serious social problems later in life: difficulty holding a job, alcohol and other drug abuse and dependency, commission of criminal or violent acts. Children who start to drink before age fifteen are much likelier to become alcoholics than those who don't drink before they turn twenty-one.

I've seen parents who are more worried that their kid will
get a disease from a mosquito bite than that their kid is out
in the woods drinking beer.

> Joanne Peterson, mother of a son who has been
> in recovery for several years and founder of Learn
> to Cope, a support group for parents of children
> addicted to opiates; Joanne's son became addicted
> to OxyContin after a friend's father gave it to him.

As is the case with respect to smoking, young teens who are heavy,
frequent drinkers are more likely to be experiencing emotional, social,
or behavioral problems, such as anxiety, depression, conduct disorders, and antisocial behavior. If this is the case with your child, your
child will need your help addressing the underlying issue in order to
stop drinking.

When it comes to reducing the likelihood of teen drinking and
binge drinking, you can make a real difference. Keep track of the
alcohol in your own home; you may even consider locking it up. See
and talk to your children (and, if you're suspicious, smell their breath)
when they return from a night out with friends. Make it clear that
drinking and driving, or being in a car with a driver who has been
drinking, is absolutely prohibited; let your children know you will
always provide a safe ride home if they ever need it.

THE DEBATE ABOUT ALLOWING
YOUR TEEN TO DRINK AT HOME

The public health message is: It is not okay for children to drink alcohol at all until they are adults, and then only in moderation. While all
states prohibit selling or furnishing alcohol to anyone under twenty-
one, most states make an exception that allows parents to provide

alcohol to their children in their homes or (in some states) in a public place.

But as a parent, you may be conflicted about what rules you should set about your teens' drinking with the family. You may wonder if all teen drinking is bad. What about small amounts at family celebrations, or at Christmas dinner? Will allowing them to drink small amounts with you teach your children to drink moderately as adults?

I will provide you with some parenting examples to consider, but how you set limits on alcohol depends very much on your knowledge of the effect of alcohol on your teen and your assessment of what will work best for your child.

Some parents believe that the best way to teach their children to use alcohol responsibly as adults is to start teaching them to drink responsibly when they are young. Parents may begin giving their children watered-down wine or small sips of beer in the tween or early teen years, gradually increasing the portion to half a glass of wine at special dinners or at family celebrations when their children are in their late teens. Parents who embrace this approach generally believe

---

While most of us are not genetically predisposed to become addicted to alcohol, there is no way of knowing whether or not any individual teenager does have this predisposition. I was a raging alcoholic by the age of fourteen, despite my parents' European attitude toward wine with dinner and sips for children. Social drinking at a dinner table with your parents doesn't necessarily affect what you'll do as a teen at parties with your friends.

Comment, "Can Sips at Home Prevent Binges?" posted on the *New York Times* website, March 26, 2008

---

that their children will learn to drink responsibly as adults if they practice limited drinking at home as teens.

There is no scientific research to support the idea that allowing your children to drink at home will prevent them from binge drinking outside the home. In Europe, many countries have no minimum drinking age; in those that do, the minimum age is usually between sixteen and eighteen. Studies have shown that in virtually every European country except Turkey (which is Muslim) teens binge drink at higher rates than in the United States. The rate of binge drinking among teens in Ireland, Germany, the UK, and Switzerland is more than twice the rate of binge drinking among teens in the U.S. The rate in Denmark is even higher.

Some parents believe that it is better to have the kids drinking under their roof than to have them drinking and driving. Other parents may be unable or unwilling to assert authority over their teens.

In 2002, Elisa Kelly's son Ryan asked her to buy beer and wine for his sixteenth-birthday party at the family's Virginia home, promising that no one would leave until morning. Kelly agreed, and to further guard against drunken driving, she collected guests' car keys. But neighbors called police, who arrested Kelly and her ex-husband, George Robinson, for what one official told *The Washington Post* was the worst case of underage drinking he'd seen in years. Kelly maintained that she was just trying to control drinking that would have gone on whether or not she had bought alcohol for the kids. Both got time in jail; Kelly began her twenty-seven-month sentence on June 11 [2007].

Barbara Kantrowitz and Anne Underwood, "The Teen Drinking Dilemma," *Newsweek*, June 25, 2007

No matter what the reason, parents who are overly permissive, or who encourage teen drinking, put their children at risk. Teens who believe that their parents will not care if they are caught drinking are more likely to drink, binge drink, and use other substances.

Another belief that underlies permissive parenting practices is that forbidding alcohol entirely will only encourage teens to drink more and to drink clandestinely. There is no evidence that letting your children drink at home will discourage them from drinking elsewhere. Nor is there any evidence that telling your teenager that he is not allowed to drink will encourage him to do the opposite.

Allowing other parents' children to drink alcohol in your home is likely to violate one or more "social host" laws. These laws, which many local jurisdictions are enacting, hold persons who are over twenty-one criminally responsible for such underage drinking that occurs in their home.

As a parent, you can learn all the facts about alcohol, but parenting is really about doing what's best for your kid. Your child is a precious individual, not a statistic. It is your job to decide what rules will work for you and your family. In making the decision regarding what message to give your children on alcohol, consider your long-term objectives. When it comes to drinking, it is more important that your children don't damage their brains, become addicted, or accidentally kill themselves by drinking too much than that they think of you as a cool parent. For every year that you're able to postpone your child's first use of alcohol, your child's risk of becoming dependent on alcohol goes down.

While I can't tell you what rules will work best for your teen, I recommend that you set clear limits that teens should not use alcohol, or at least not unless they are drinking on some special occasion with you, stick to those limits when your teen pushes against them, and enforce them with consequences when your teen violates them.

Realistically, it may be difficult to prevent your teen from ever drinking alcohol. Your teen is prone to risk-taking. This is normal teenage behavior. Even if you expect that your child will drink underage, don't make it easy for him to do so. CASA research shows that teens who are closely monitored and supervised, who believe that their parents will catch and punish them if they are caught drinking, are less likely to drink. In fact, teens want their parents to establish and enforce limits. Despite any protest otherwise, remember: Your teen really does want you to be a parent.

If you decide to allow your child to try alcohol under your supervision, a little wine at Christmas or a family celebration, you should take steps to ensure that your child is not drinking outside your home without your supervision.

MARIJUANA: THE MOST UNDERESTIMATED DRUG

If you used marijuana when you were young, you may consider smoking pot a harmless high, or you may fear appearing hypocritical if you tell your child not to do it. Perhaps you see using marijuana as a rite of passage, a phase your teen will pass through unharmed on the way to becoming an adult.

You shouldn't be blasé about blazing blunts or bongs. Things have changed since you were a teenager. As is the case with cigarettes, we know a lot more about marijuana today than we did a generation ago. Moreover, today's marijuana is a much more potent and dangerous drug than the pot of the 1970s or 1980s. The pot that your child would be offered today is likely to be as much as ten times more powerful than the marijuana available a generation ago. We've still got a lot to learn about the consequences of smoking marijuana, but what we now know tells us that it's dangerous for your child to use it.

Marijuana, even in small amounts, causes a loss of physical coordination and a deterioration of motor skills. Marijuana is second only to

Steve Kelley

alcohol as the most frequently detected psychoactive substance among impaired drivers who are involved in accidents.

We also know that marijuana can adversely affect your child's memory, ability to learn and concentrate, and neurological and emotional development. The impact on memory and decision-making

There is no question that marijuana can be addictive; that argument is over. The most important thing right now is to understand the vulnerability of young developing brains to these increased concentrations of cannabis.

Nora Volkow, MD, director, National
Institute on Drug Abuse

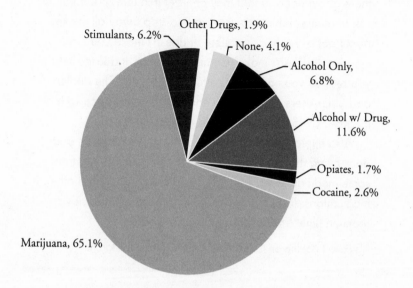

**Treatment Admissions by Primary Substance
of Abuse, Ages 12 to 17**

Other Drugs, 1.9%

Stimulants, 6.2%

None, 4.1%

Alcohol Only,
6.8%

Alcohol w/ Drug,
11.6%

Opiates, 1.7%

Cocaine, 2.6%

Marijuana, 65.1%

SAMHSA Treatment Episode Data Set (2005)

is especially significant for teens, whose brains and bodies are still developing. If children smoke pot, even just on the weekends, it is likely to affect their ability to learn and perform well in school.

We now know that marijuana can be addictive, and that adolescents are more vulnerable to becoming dependent on marijuana than adults. Indeed, the number of teens entering drug treatment for problems with marijuana has been rising sharply—among teens under eighteen there are almost twice as many treatment admissions for marijuana as the primary substance of abuse than for alcohol and all other drugs combined.

Heavy teenage marijuana smokers show reduced brain matter and other cognitive defects later in life. If your children smoke marijuana regularly, they will likely suffer from many of the same respiratory

They [kids] know that there is a ton of false information out there about pot and that they can get it in fifth grade if they ask at recess! I think it's important to strip away all the lies about pot as early as possible. It doesn't make you more creative, it doesn't make you more popular, it doesn't help you rest, so you can study better . . . etc., etc. The dealers and older users are going to come at them full force with the REASONS why they should use.

Also explain that it does affect the nervous system and does numb the body and that is why people use it to treat some medical issues, but they could just as easily use other medications. It shuts down the nerve receptors and slows reaction time! That is dangerous, not good!

Parent posting on CASA Parent Power discussion forum

problems as tobacco smokers, including chronic bronchitis, coughing, wheezing, chest sounds, and increased phlegm.

More frighteningly, recent research has shown a possible relationship between marijuana and the onset of psychotic episodes in people who have certain genetic factors that predispose them to mental illness. If your family has a history of mental illness, tell your children how this makes it even more important to stay clear of marijuana; there's a chance that it could trigger the mental illness.

The best way to keep your children away from marijuana is to send a clear message that smoking pot is unacceptable and explain the reasons why. You can use the facts in this chapter to explain how marijuana is dangerous to both health and safety, interrupts brain development, and may prevent your child from succeeding in school and life. Plus, it's illegal.

Most important, if you catch your kids smoking pot, don't let it slide: You should nip the bud in the bud. Setting boundaries and enforcing consequences is the key to raising healthy children. Punishing your children will not make them hate you, it will teach them that smoking marijuana is not okay. In Chapter 14, "The Signs of Use—What to Do If You See Them," I provide specific suggestions for parenting steps to take if you discover that your child is smoking marijuana.

PRESCRIPTION DRUGS: THE NEW BULLY ON THE BLOCK

Kids swap prescription pills at the lunch table. They mostly trade OxyContin and Adderall, because they're easier to get.

Fourteen-year-old student quoted in "Pill Swapping," *Teen Vogue*, November 2007

Like alcohol, prescription drugs are likely to be available in your home. If there aren't any in your medicine cabinet, you can bet that some parents of your children's classmates keep them around the house, or that your children's friends are being prescribed medicine by doctors and sharing it with others.

Teenagers are abusing prescription drugs to get high at alarming rates. They host teen "pharming" parties, where bowls of pills may be

Mobile County Public Schools in Alabama reported six on-campus pharming parties last year, including one involving a fifth grader.

ABC News, September 12, 2006

offered like M&Ms. Some students pass pills like notes in the classroom. Prescription drugs have become the fourth most commonly abused substance among teens—behind alcohol, tobacco, and marijuana. Sadly, the growing epidemic of prescription drug abuse shows no signs of abating, and the incidence of deaths caused by prescription drug overdoses continues to rise.

As a parent, in order to protect your children from the risks of abuse, you need to know the facts about prescription drugs—what they are, why children are taking them, and how children are obtaining them.

There are three kinds of prescription drugs that the federal government controls because of the potential for their abuse: painkillers, depressants, and stimulants.

Painkillers, which can be highly addictive, are used by doctors to treat serious and chronic pain (caused by a surgery, an accident, or a disease, such as cancer). Commonly abused painkillers include OxyContin, Vicodin, fentanyl, Darvon, Dilaudid, codeine, Demerol, Percocet, and Percodan. The vast majority of teens who abuse prescription drugs abuse painkillers. Properly used, OxyContin is time-released to provide relief over many hours; teens crunch them up to break the time release seal and get the full dose at once, creating a rush.

There are two kinds of depressants. The most commonly abused depressants are tranquilizers, which are generally used to treat anxi-

---

"[Adderall] abuse can make you paranoid and crazy," Ivan K. Goldberg, a Manhattan psychopharmacologist, says of improper usage, adding that addiction, rapid heartbeat, and insomnia are other side effects.

Deborah Schoeneman, "Focus Factor: Adderall is the new recreational Ritalin. But is it safe?" *New York*, May 10, 2004

In Florida, one of few states that closely tracks prescription drug overdoses, in 2007 the rate of deaths caused by such drugs was more than three times the rate of deaths caused by all illegal drugs combined. Cocaine, heroin, and all methylated amphetamines caused 989 deaths, while legal opioids (painkillers like Vicodin and OxyContin) caused 2,328. Drugs with benzodiazepine, mainly depressants like Valium and Xanax, led to 743 deaths.

"Drugs Identified in Deceased Persons by
Florida Medical Examiners," 2007 Report

ety, and include medications such as diazepam (Valium), Temazepam, and Xanax. The other kind of depressant is a sedative, which is generally used to induce sleep, and includes Nembutal and Membaral. Both kinds are addictive. The effects of depressants can linger, and will affect cognition and memory; students who abuse them may see their grades suffer.

Stimulants, which are also addictive, are used to treat a variety of medical disorders, including asthma, respiratory problems, obesity, attention deficit/hyperactivity disorder (ADHD), and narcolepsy. Benzedrine, Ritalin, Dexedrine, and Adderall are all brand names of stimulants. Ritalin and Adderall are commonly prescribed to treat ADHD in children, and are the stimulants most commonly prescribed to teens and most often abused by them.

Teen prescription drug abuse is fueled by ready availability and misconceptions about the safety of such drugs.

Among teens, the abuse of prescription drugs carries much less stigma than abuse of other substances. Most teenagers think that prescription drugs aren't dangerous. Half of them think that prescription drugs are much safer than other drugs, and one-third incorrectly think that prescription drugs aren't addictive. After all, teens observe

> The synthetic opiates (OxyContin, Vicodin) that are widely abused are . . . not only a source of addiction, but they . . . can be a source of seizure, even death, when taken in quantities.
>
> White House Office of National Drug Control Policy

doctors prescribing these drugs to patients, including teens' own parents and friends, so they think (mistakenly), "How dangerous can these drugs be?"

You and your children need to understand that abusing prescription drugs is at least as dangerous as abusing other drugs. Abuse of prescription drugs can lead to addiction, serious emotional, social, and health problems, medical emergencies, and death. Like marijuana use, prescription drug abuse can lead to other drug use. Teens who pop prescription pills for fun are much more likely to try or use other drugs than teens who don't. Indeed, teens who are hooked on Oxy-Contin will sometimes switch to heroin if they can't obtain or afford the pills, because they can get a stronger, cheaper high with heroin.

Taken in large doses, or when mixed together or with other drugs, prescription drugs can be a recipe for tragedy. In 2006, nearly half of all drug-related emergency room visits involved the abuse of prescription drugs. Teach your child that whenever people use prescription

> In the past fifteen years, there has been a 3,196 percent increase in the number of deaths caused by mixing prescription drugs with alcohol and/or street drugs.
>
> David P. Phillips, et al., "A Steep Increase in Domestic Fatal Medication Errors with Use of Alcohol and/or Street Drugs," Archives of Internal Medicine, July 28, 2008

drugs without a doctor's supervision, they are putting themselves at risk of serious harm.

Let your children know that you view their abuse of prescription drugs the same way you view other drug use, and that the same consequences will apply if you catch them doing it. As with alcohol and marijuana, don't let it slide if you discover that your teen is abusing prescription drugs. In Chapter 14, "The Signs of Use—What to Do If You See Them," I suggest steps to take if you suspect or discover that your child is abusing prescription drugs.

KEEP CONTROLLED PRESCRIPTION DRUGS AWAY FROM CHILDREN

One factor driving the increase in prescription drug abuse is how easily these drugs can be acquired from doctors, friends, relatives, classmates, and the Internet. For many teens, prescription drugs are easier to get than beer.

With the click of a mouse, teenagers can purchase all sorts of highly addictive controlled prescription drugs on the Internet without a prescription: All they need is a credit card. Indeed, the Internet is a pharmaceutical candy store. Prescription drugs can be purchased in your home, right under your nose, free from the scrutiny of parents, medical professionals, or law enforcement.

As a parent, you play a key role in limiting your child's access to prescription drugs. Don't leave controlled prescription pills around the house or in places where children can find them. Carefully dispose of unused pills. Monitor the pills in your medicine cabinet; lock it if necessary. Your carelessness can yield inadvertent but devastating harm to your own children. Make sure you monitor your child's use of the Internet and check your credit-card bill for unidentified, innocuous-looking purchases. They may be drug purchases.

You have the Parent Power and parental responsibility to decrease your child's access to pills. Talk to your child about the risks of abusing prescription drugs, and address any underlying issues that might cause your child to use.

TEEN ATHLETES AND STEROIDS

Is your teen an athlete? If so, you probably appreciate the pressure your teen is under to perform, especially if he or she is competing for a college scholarship. You may also be personally invested in your teen's athletic activities—attending practices and competitions, arranging car pools, and cooking special meals. Amongst all the activity, make sure you make time to talk to your teen about the dangers of steroids.

The explosion in steroid use among high school and college athletes is linked to teens' admiration and emulation of professional athletes. Some of our most cherished athletes—baseball stars like Alex "A-Rod" Rodriguez and Barry Bonds, and track and cycling stars—who have broken world records used steroids to accomplish their feats.

Teens who witness the adulation accorded these athletes may conclude that "juicing" is an acceptable way to gain an advantage over the competition. Plus, the pressure on teen athletes to perform has

---

From 1991 to 2007, the number of girls aged 12–18 using steroids has increased by 182 percent, from 138,330 to 390,353; the number of boys aged 12–18 using steroids is up 55 percent, from 498,184 to 774,739.

U.S. Department of Health & Human Services,
Centers for Disease Control and Prevention,
Youth Risk Behavior Surveillance System

---

increased as getting into college has become much more competitive and scholarships have become so critical to defray high tuitions.

In order to steer your children away from steroids, you need to appreciate what they are and why kids use them.

Steroids are synthetic copies of the naturally occurring male hormone testosterone. Steroids are used to treat medical conditions that result when the body's normal levels of testosterone are too low (e.g., body wasting in patients with AIDS). The doses that athletes use are ten to one hundred times stronger than the doses used to treat medical conditions.

Why do teens use steroids? Teens use steroids to boost their performance, increase their strength and stamina, or enhance their physical appearance. They may feel pressure from their coach, other teammates, or even from a parent to do whatever it takes to succeed. Teens can be impulsive, and see steroids as a quick fix to bulking up. Some teen athletes hit a plateau and think that steroids will take them to the next level. In addition to performance enhancement, girls may use steroids to improve their appearance, "get cut," lose body fat, and reduce breast size. This body sculpting may account for the huge increase in steroid use among girls.

Simply explaining the unattractive side effects may be enough to persuade your teen not to try steroids. To your son, explain that steroids can take away his masculinity—he may lose his hair, his sperm count may go down, his testicles may shrink, he might grow breasts, and he could develop severe acne. To your daughter, explain that her voice may get deep like a man's, her breasts may shrink, she may grow dark facial hair, and get severe acne. Long-term use of steroids by either men or women can cause liver damage and heart disease.

Your teen may not realize that steroids can be addictive, and may underestimate the emotional side effects, which can be devastating. While on steroids, your teen may experience delusions or "roid rage," an increased aggression that leads to fights and hostility. Roid rage

For years, Rob Garibaldi was told that he had all the ingredients of a major league baseball player except size, so he started using steroids to gain the bulk he needed to make the big time. He was drafted by the New York Yankees. When he stopped using steroids so he would be clean for his physical, he became depressed and violent and suffered wild hallucinations. When his mother and father discovered that he had been using steroids, he said he was just modeling himself after his heroes, Barry Bonds and Mark McGwire.

The price, in [his father] Raymond Garibaldi's words, was "mania, depression, short-term memory loss, uncontrollable rage, delusional and suicidal thinking, and paranoid psychosis." In a spiral of suicidal depression kicked off by his steroid use, Rob Garibaldi shot himself in the head with a .357 Magnum pistol at the age of twenty-four.

Associated Press, March 17, 2005

behavior can be serious enough to get your teen kicked off the team or thrown out of school. When a teen stops taking steroids, the withdrawal can cause a depression so severe that some have committed suicide.

Reassure your teen that your love and support is not conditioned on athletic success. Also, explain that long-term health is more important than the short-term gains of winning.

Discuss how an athlete's integrity is compromised by using performance-enhancing drugs. You can cite examples of athletes who have been dethroned by steroids. Marion Jones's doping forced her entire relay team to give back their Olympic gold medals. Floyd Landis was stripped of his Tour de France victory and dropped from the Phonak team after failing a drug test. Such stories illustrate that using drugs to excel in sports is ultimately cheating, and that it can hurt not only the athlete but the entire team.

Talk to your child's coach about your expectations that the students not use steroids. See that the coach is sending the same message to the kids.

Make sure your teen understands that the real recipe for success is making a long-term commitment to eating a healthy diet, getting enough sleep, and maintaining a rigorous training schedule.

PARENT TIPS

- Give your child a clear message that tobacco, alcohol, marijuana, and abusable prescription drugs are dangerous and prohibited.
- Educate your child about the dangers of teen drinking, binge drinking, and drinking and driving.
- See and talk to your child upon returning from a night out; if suspicious, when hugging your teen, smell his breath.
- Dispel the myth that marijuana use is harmless.
- Discuss the dangers of abusing prescription drugs, including overdose and addiction, with your child.
- Keep track of prescription drugs; don't allow them to fall into the hands of your child.
- Monitor your child's use of the Internet.
- Alert your teen to the dangers of steroid use.

5

FOR YOUR TEEN,
AVAILABILITY IS
THE MOTHER OF USE

YOUR CHILD'S WORLD IS FULL OF DRUGS

Understanding the world your child lives in is essential. I'm going to
describe that world for you. Better sit down while you read this.

Are drugs available to kids everywhere? You bet they are. Today's
teens are exposed daily to a dizzying menu of addictive illegal and
prescription drugs, glamorously advertised cigarettes, beer, wine coolers, fruit-flavored hard liquors, malternatives, candy-flavored chewing
tobacco, and inhalants.

Wherever you live—large city or small town, affluent suburb or
rural community, the North, South, East, or West—the substances
sure to be within easy reach for your kids are tobacco, alcohol, marijuana, and prescription pills. Some other drugs are likelier to show up
in some parts of the country. Methamphetamine is more prevalent

in the West and Far West, and in Wyoming and North and South Dakota. Teens in some cities in Texas have gotten into "cheese," a potent, sometimes flavored mix of heroin and an over-the-counter medicine. Crack cocaine is widely available in poor sections of major eastern cities. Powder cocaine is likelier to be available in affluent areas. Teens are abusing painkillers more frequently in Washington, Kentucky, Oregon, Michigan, and Oklahoma. Tranquilizers are more popular among teens in southern states like Arkansas, North Carolina, Tennessee, Louisiana, Florida, and South Carolina.

There will also be times when some drugs are cheaper or more available than others. Heroin, for example, has fluctuated in price over the decades, but in recent years it is cheaper in some communities than a movie ticket. Powder cocaine tends to be expensive, but in its crack form it is well within the weekly allowances of most kids.

AVAILABILITY IS THE MOTHER OF USE

Casual and frequent exposure makes experimentation tempting. Surely your teenage son or daughter has uttered these words to you at some point in his or her life: "But all my friends are doing it! Even [insert the name of straightlaced best friend who hangs out at your house after school all the time] is doing it!" Perhaps that argument was made to you in support of drinking at a party or smoking a little pot. Maybe you've even learned from other parents in your community or teachers at your child's school that yes, in fact a lot of kids are drinking or smoking or indulging in a little drug experimentation. You may think that because this kind of behavior is relatively common in your area, it is harmless. Think again.

Teen alcohol and other drug use is risky business—risky for your kid's physical and mental health and well-being in the present day, and risky for their future, since the younger kids are when they start to use, the likelier they are to develop addictions. Our advice to you is the same you might give to your child: Just because others—your friends, your classmates—are doing it doesn't mean it's okay.

The reality is that the vast majority of teens are not using illegal drugs. National surveys suggest that about 38 percent of high-schoolers have tried marijuana; less than 8 percent of high school students have tried cocaine, meth, or heroin. That is the good news. The bad news, however, is that teen drinking is widespread, and marijuana, prescription drugs, and alcohol are readily available to teens. Resistance is an ongoing battle.

Many factors drive teen decision-making about using substances, but economics and convenience are among the most important. These are factors in why government laws and policies have imposed taxes to increase the price of cigarettes, enforced underage-purchasing bans, and prohibited indoor smoking. These steps have proven effective in driving youth smoking rates down because the more expensive and harder it is to smoke, and the less socially acceptable, the less likely kids are to do it.

In CASA's survey, we ask teens every year to rate beer, cigarettes, marijuana, and prescription drugs by the ease with which they can buy them. Cigarettes are easiest for your kids to buy, but marijuana is a close second. In the past, beer was third and prescription drugs were fourth, but in 2008 more teens reported that prescription drugs are easier to buy than beer.

Every year we ask the teens we survey: "If you wanted to buy marijuana right now, how long would it take you?" In 2008, 42 percent of twelve- to seventeen-year-olds could get it within a day; and 23 percent could get it within an hour. That means almost eleven million teens have ready access to the drug, and six million would need only one hour to obtain it. The following chart illustrates this point.

**If you wanted to buy marijuana right now, how
long would it take you to get it?**

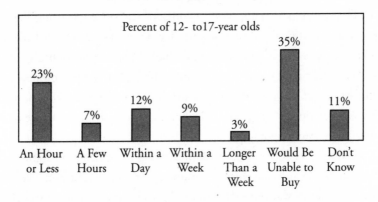

CASA. *National Survey of American Attitudes on Substance
Abuse XIII: Teens and Parents (2008)*

WHERE DO TEENS GET DRUGS?

When you think about how teens obtain drugs, you may picture a kid sneaking down a back alley to make a purchase from a street drug dealer. But in reality kids get drugs in the most run-of-the-mill places, the places where they spend most of their time: their homes, their schools, and their friends' homes. Teens can get the nation's two legal drugs—cigarettes and alcohol—from adults or older friends. A government survey found that 40 percent of underage drinkers were given alcohol for free by an adult in the prior month. Teens can also purchase cigarettes and alcohol from careless, inattentive, or unscrupulous retailers and bartenders or by using fake IDs.

In the Home

Parents stock a wide variety of substances in their homes—from addictive painkillers in the bathroom medicine cabinet to inhalants in aerosol canisters under the kitchen sink, beer in the refrigerator, and liquor in the living room. Most underage drinking goes on in homes. Half of underage drinkers had their last drink in a friend's home, another 30 percent in their own home.

Teens and tweens sometimes inhale the fumes of common household supplies—glue, cleaning fluid, spray paint—in order to get high. These products are toxic and their abuse can damage the heart, lungs, liver, kidneys, and brain. Also abused by tweens and teens are over-the-counter drugs, such as cough medicines and decongestants, which can be psychologically addictive and fatal if combined with other drugs.

Two generations ago, parents locked up their liquor so their kids could not get at it. In today's world, the family medicine cabinet is filled with Adderall, Ritalin, Valium, and Vicodin, which can be at least as tempting as alcohol to teens looking for a high. It is important to explain to your teen the dangers of those drugs and to keep them out of reach and out of temptation. At the very least, keep count of pills like OxyContin if you are taking them to relieve severe pain,

---

Special Agent Gerard P. McAleer, in charge of the DEA in New Jersey, gives talks about how teenagers often steal prescription drugs from relatives. "A woman came to me with tears in her eyes. She said that until that moment she never realized how her daughter got hooked on prescription painkillers. She told me that she had actually been proud that her daughter had wanted to spend so much time visiting her grandmother, who was dying from cancer. The grandmother had been prescribed the painkiller fentanyl."

Ed Johnson, "Prescription for Abuse of Potent Drugs," *Asbury Park Press*, June 22, 2008

and discard pills you no longer use. In some situations, it may even be necessary to lock the family medicine cabinet.

In Schools

From August or September to May or June, your teen is spending a large part of his or her waking hours at school. If it's a high school, odds are that drugs are used, kept, or sold there. That sad fact is also true of up to a third of middle schools. Teens who see drugs in their schools are much likelier to be able to obtain them quickly. Compared to teens who do not see drugs at their schools, those who do are four times likelier to be able to buy marijuana within a day and nearly six times likelier to be able to buy marijuana within an hour.

For you, the bottom line is that each weekday during those school months, your son or daughter may be in an environment where it's easy to get drugs. This means that you need to understand the school world of your teen. Understanding that environment—and your potential to change it—is so important that I have devoted Chapter 12, "How Can I Protect My Kids at School?" to the subject.

If a health inspector discovered that there were toxic substances behind the walls of your middle and high school that would, over time, result in chronic, debilitating diseases for anywhere from 9 to 32 percent of the students who came into contact with them—and lead to a premature death for some of them—can you imagine the public uproar that would ensue?

Thom Forbes, parent and creator of *The Elephant on Main Street*, an interactive memoir of addiction and recovery

THE ADOLESCENT BRAIN AND DRUGS

Why is it that your teenager at times seems to be so impulsive, so reckless? Why do teens sometimes appear to behave as if they are immortal, impervious to harm? Because teenagers' brains are still developing. The process of cognitive development that started early in the womb continues well into the mid-twenties, when the human brain becomes fully formed. Teenagers may look like grown-ups, and some seem to be as smart as grown-ups, but because their brains are still maturing, they don't have the ability to control impulses the way grown-ups do.

Through adolescence and into early adulthood, the areas of the brain that regulate cognitive and emotional behavior go through a "remodeling" process. The parts of the brain responsible for self-regulation (such as understanding long-term consequences and controlling impulsive behaviors) begin developing at this stage and aren't complete until early adulthood, around age twenty-five. Because their brains are still developing, adolescents lack some of the "wiring" that sends the brake or stop messages to the rest of the brain. This makes adolescents and young adults more prone to engage in risky behaviors such as smoking, drinking, and illegal drug use. Teenagers' brains

Unfortunately kids don't pull their hands away from drugs and alcohol because they don't get burned immediately. So they are left to grapple with the issue: What feels good often isn't good for you.

Priscilla Dann-Courtney, psychologist and parent

encourage them to take risks for fun, and don't perceive those risks as dangerous in the way that adult brains do.

WHY DRUG USE LEADS TO MORE DRUG USE

You've probably heard mention of the gateway relationship among cigarettes, alcohol, marijuana, and other drugs. This refers to the fact that kids who smoke cigarettes and drink alcohol are more likely to use marijuana than those who don't, and kids who smoke marijuana are far more likely to use drugs like cocaine, meth, hallucinogens, and heroin than those who don't.

Your teen—and even some parents—will point out that not all kids who smoke cigarettes will drink alcohol (and vice versa), that most kids who smoke cigarettes and drink alcohol will not use marijuana, and that most kids who smoke marijuana will not move on to drugs like cocaine, meth, heroin, and hallucinogens.

That's true. But fostering good health in your children means teaching them to avoid behaviors that increase their risk of substance abuse and addiction. For some time we at CASA have been identifying the statistical relationship among use of these substances:

• Most teens who use marijuana first smoked cigarettes or drank alcohol.

- Teens who use marijuana are much likelier than teens who don't to use cocaine.
- Teens who begin smoking cigarettes by age twelve are likelier than nonsmokers to be binge drinkers and to become alcohol- and marijuana-dependent.
- Teens who abuse prescription drugs are twice as likely to use alcohol, five times more likely to use marijuana, twelve times more likely to use heroin, fifteen times more likely to use ecstasy, and twenty-one times more likely to use cocaine, compared to teens who do not abuse such drugs.

To put this in perspective, in 1964 the first Surgeon General's Report on smoking found a nine to ten times greater risk of lung cancer among smokers, and early results of the extensive Framingham heart study found that individuals with high cholesterol were two to four times likelier to suffer heart disease. Most kids who smoke marijuana do not move on to other drugs, just as most people who smoke cigarettes do not develop lung cancer; but both kinds of smokers enormously increase their risks.

Parents who ignore these relationships among addictive substances are playing Russian roulette with their children. Virtually all cocaine users smoked cigarettes, drank alcohol, and smoked pot first. Seventeen percent of adolescents who try illicit drugs start with inhalants. If your child has started using alcohol or marijuana, he is likelier to try other drugs than a child who hasn't been drinking or smoking pot.

Nicotine is much more of a "gateway" drug than marijuana. More kids initiate drug use with nicotine than with marijuana. If you're a smoker, that increases the risk of marijuana use and in turn the risk of other drugs.

Nora Volkow, MD, National Institute on Drug Abuse

One reason some teens who smoke or drink move on to other drugs is that they have a behavioral and/or emotional problem, such as oppositional defiant disorder (ODD) or conduct disorder, which causes them to act out and be rebellious. For these teens, drinking or drug use may be part of a larger cluster of negative, antisocial, or destructive behaviors. As I point out in Chapter 7, "In What Circumstances Is My Child at Increased Risk of Drug Use?" children with conduct disorders are likelier to get into substance abuse.

Genetic factors can sometimes explain why a teen moves from smoking and drinking to use of marijuana and other drugs. The social situation may also be a factor. Children trying different drugs or pills may suggest that they try each other's illegal drug or prescription pill.

Another reason drug use leads to more drug use is neurological. It has to do with how drugs affect the brain. If you've ever been on a low-sugar diet, like Atkins or South Beach, you probably learned that eating sugar makes you crave more sugar. Processed sugar (the kind you find in sweets) is, in many ways, just like a drug. Your body doesn't need it. It's not good for you, and the more you eat it, the more you want it. So it is with drugs—when you put any drug in your body, your body craves more drugs, and over time, it craves larger doses and more intense drugs.

In recent years, scientists have identified a likely explanation for this relationship. All of the substances of abuse—nicotine, alcohol, marijuana, cocaine, heroin, methamphetamine, and opioids—increase the levels of dopamine in the brain. Dopamine is the chemical messenger that produces feelings of pleasure and excitement; it is released in the brain in response to a rewarding experience (e.g., eating delicious food). Dopamine is believed to be a teaching signal that helps the brain learn to repeat behaviors that are rewarding—in the case of drugs, reinforcing drug-taking behavior.

Whatever the substance, the brains of drug users are "rewired," becoming predisposed to cravings. These adaptations may happen more quickly, and more profoundly, for some drugs. For example, nicotine has actually been shown to create especially rapid changes in the pleasure/reward pathways in the brain. The changes caused by one drug increase the brain's sensitivity to other drugs—in effect, the drug creates a primer for further and faster changes by other drugs.

Long-term abuse of alcohol and other substances can also rewire the pleasure/reward system of the brain so that normal pleasurable activities that used to stimulate these pathways (e.g., winning at sports, eating good food, achieving goals) are no longer sufficient. As a result, the only way the addict's brain can increase dopamine levels and experience resulting pleasure is by using drugs. The more frequently and longer an addict uses drugs, the more drugs that addict needs to create the high.

When you tell this to your teen, he might well say, "I know lots of kids who smoke pot and they never use any of those dangerous drugs like heroin." At that point, go to the NIDA website, search for "Drugs, Brains, and Behavior—The Science of Addiction" (www.nida.nih.gov/scienceofaddiction/brain.html), and show him how each of the substances affects and disrupts the functioning of the same parts of the brain. Then ask him: "Why take an unnecessary risk, one that could mess up your brain and destroy your life?"

Drugs also change the teenage brain in ways that can make the brain more susceptible to addiction later. The neurological damage created by drug use during adolescence disrupts the pleasure/reward centers in such a way that the brain learns to become addicted. The result is that teenagers who abuse substances are much more susceptible to developing chronic substance-abuse problems later in life.

What does all this brain science mean for you as a parent? Adolescent passions are normal, and can be healthy, so long as they are directed in the right ways. Help to ensure that your teen's natural propensity for risk taking and pleasure seeking leads him or her to get involved in healthy activities like sports, arts, music, drama, social, political or religious causes, or achieving academic success.

You can help your teens understand that experimenting with drugs at an early age can change their brains permanently. To the extent that your teens grasp this, it will make it easier for you to guide them to make smart decisions and even appreciate the long-term risks and consequences of drug use.

PARENT TIPS

- Learn which drugs are more prevalent in your community and discuss avoiding those drugs with your children.
- Make sure that inhalants, cigarettes, alcohol, and prescription drugs are not easily accessible in your home.
- Educate your children about how the teen brain is particularly vulnerable to the damaging and addictive effects of alcohol and other drugs.

6

AT WHAT TIMES IS
MY CHILD AT INCREASED
RISK OF DRUG USE?

There is no one-size-fits-all approach to raising healthy, drug-free children. Like each mother and each father, each child is unique—in personality, strengths and weaknesses, needs and wants, emotions and learning styles. Knowing each of your children, who they are, what makes them tick, and what makes them feel good (or bad) about themselves, will help you reduce their risk of substance abuse.

There are some risk factors that you should look out for. In this chapter and the next, I will describe the times, characteristics, and situations that can increase the danger that any child will smoke, drink, or use drugs. Being able to spot these, providing appropriate support, and taking timely action to modify your child's behavior can reduce the chances that your child will use tobacco, alcohol, or other drugs.

At certain times in your child's life, the risk of smoking, drinking, and abusing illegal or prescription drugs will increase. As the song and psalm say, "To everything there is a season," and there are times when adolescents are more likely to try drugs. During these times you should be vigilant and remind your children of your rules and expectations about substance abuse.

Just being a teenager in America today is a risk factor for experimenting with addictive substances. Our society showers tweens and teens with enticements to smoke, drink, and use drugs: advertising on television and radio, in magazines and websites, stories about entertainment and sports celebrities, television shows and movies glamorizing smoking, drinking, and drug use, and the conduct of other teens at their schools or in their neighborhoods.

Timing for teens can be everything: In the span of a few months, a teen's attitude toward smoking, drinking, or illegal drug use can change dramatically. Indeed, entertainment outlets, such as the cable channel MTV, repeatedly survey teens and preteens to keep up with changing attitudes and tastes.

During any or all of the transition times described in this chapter, your children's attitudes about tobacco, alcohol, and other drugs may change. If you are on the lookout for these changes, you can provide appropriate support, encouragement, and discipline. And you can take needed actions—such as getting to know your child's new friends and their parents, monitoring your child's whereabouts, and finding out about the parties your kids are attending—in order to help your child get through these risky times unscathed.

ENTERING MIDDLE SCHOOL

The first several months of middle school tend to be a time when a child's view of substance abuse can significantly shift. Prior to that time, while at home, in preschool and in lower school, children tend to develop strong antismoking, antidrinking, and antidrugging attitudes. They may see all such conduct as wrong and harmful, something that they would never do. If you smoke, drink, or use drugs, your children are likely to urge you to stop, and their classmates will almost surely share their disdain for such activity.

In 1975, when my son, Joe, was eleven, we were sitting on the beach in Wellfleet on Cape Cod. Since his birthday came soon after Christmas, he never got a proper present. I said, "Tell me what you want for your birthday this year, we'll get it in September when we return to Washington."

"Dad, I want you to quit smoking," he said.

"No, tell me what you really want," I responded.

"Dad, I really want you to quit smoking."

When I returned to Washington, I entered a smoking cessation program and quit that October.

As boys and girls enter middle school (fifth or sixth grade), they are exposed to the sights and sounds of substance abuse. They will see some eighth graders who are school leaders—athletes, class officers, popular kids—smoke, drink, and use marijuana. Witnessing such conduct, especially by kids they'd like to be like, or be liked by, can affect their view of substance abuse.

PUBERTY

During middle school, children start to go through puberty. Typically, girls begin puberty at an earlier age than boys. The physical changes that girls experience—gaining weight, developing breasts, menstruating, and getting zits—can be especially difficult. These physical changes can cause girls to become insecure about their looks, their bodies, and their new identities as women. As their sense of self becomes less secure, so may their sense of what they believe in.

For both boys and girls, puberty brings emotional and behavioral changes, such as increased risk taking and pleasure seeking for boys, and anxiety and depression in girls. These emotional aspects of puberty can increase the risk that your son or daughter will start

When my boys were teens and tweens, I brought a home drug test and set it on the kitchen counter. I told them that if I ever suspected any one of them of doing drugs, that I would not hesitate to test them. I told them it was not there to intimidate them, but to assure their privacy. I would test first before I began going through their things.

A local drug-enforcement officer told me it was the wisest choice I could have made because it gave my sons a valid excuse to resist peer pressure. They could respond, "Hey, I can't try that because my mom tests us at home for drug use."

Many of our friends and neighbors now use the same strategy.

Parent posting on CASA Parent Power discussion forum

experimenting with substances. Particularly for girls, early puberty may increase the risk of substance use.

Your Parent Power can influence your children's decision to resist cigarettes, alcohol, and illegal drugs during these years. Being engaged in your children's lives as they move through this period—having dinner together frequently, attending religious services together, keeping communication open, involving yourself in their after-school activities, and if at all possible having a parent or other adult present when they get home—will help keep your child drug free.

ENTERING HIGH SCHOOL

The next transition is when your children enter high school—and it's a big one: The average risk of substance abuse *triples* when students enter high school.

Children's attitudes about smoking, drinking, and using drugs often change during the first few months of high school because they are exposed to a new battery of influences. They will see classmates smoking, drinking, and taking drugs, not only marijuana, but also pills like OxyContin and Vicodin, hallucinogens, perhaps even cocaine and designer drugs. In high school, your children will learn that they can purchase these substances from classmates who seem to be "nice" guys and gals. The mix of students also changes from middle school to high school—younger kids are now exposed to older kids, whom they look up to. The younger students tend to emulate the popular older kids' riskier attitudes and behaviors.

For many teens, starting high school increases the risk of substance use because alcohol, marijuana, and pills are so available, and it is a time of stress and uncertainty for them, as they struggle to find their place in new environments and join new social groups. Adolescents begin to shift their focus from their parents and other adults, looking instead to peer and popular culture for self-evaluation and self-critique. Especially for girls, this time can be associated with less

Rob Rogers

satisfaction with physical appearance, concern about weight, increased depression, lower self-esteem, and decreased academic success—any of which can heighten the risk of substance use.

In high school, the likelihood of being offered drugs—prescription drugs, marijuana, ecstasy, and cocaine—jumps dramatically. Indeed, just about every child in America, almost certainly including yours, will be offered drugs before they graduate from high school, most on many occasions.

During the summer before and in the months after high school starts, find opportunities to reiterate your values and expectations. When you ask your children about their high school experiences— school work, social life, sports—routinely include questions about substance use: "Are the older kids drinking or smoking pot?" "How about any kids in your class?"

As your child makes new friends in high school, you should make the time to get to know them and, if possible, their parents.

THE HOURS AFTER SCHOOL

For children aged twelve to seventeen, the weekday is roughly divided into two equal parts: During school and after school. How and with whom your children spend those hours after the school bell rings are critical. Most of the smoking, alcohol, and drug use that goes on among teens occurs while kids are hanging out with one another, un-supervised by adults, after school. Knowing where your children are and ensuring they are properly supervised after school can reduce the likelihood that your children will spend that time drinking or using other drugs.

What activities students typically engage in after school is also relevant to their risk of substance abuse. Those who go home to do homework are at least risk. Those who spend some afternoons partici-pating in an extracurricular activity use drugs less often than those who are not involved in such activities. Here participation in supervised sports can be beneficial both in occupying teens after school and in building self-confidence, a sense of the importance of team work, and physical fitness.

Teens who simply hang out with their friends after school are at greatest risk, and the later they stay out with those friends, the greater the risk.

Not knowing where your child is and what your child is up to at 10:00 P.M. on a school night is risky business. Why? Because the later that teens are hanging out with friends on school nights, the likelier it is that drug and alcohol use will be going on among them. Half of twelve- to seventeen-year-olds that come home after 10:00 P.M. say that's the case, as do almost a third of those who come home between 8:00 P.M. and 10:00 P.M.

The old public service message, "It's 10:00 P.M., do you know where your children are?" gets the point across, but it doesn't go far enough. Whether your children are at the mall, hanging out in the park, or at their best friend's house, if grown-ups aren't around, alcohol and drugs may be. The more important question to ask yourself is: "Are my children being supervised by a responsible adult?"

No sleepovers—none—for our daughters once they were in high school.

Parent posting on CASA Parent Power discussion forum

Do not allow your children to invite friends over when you're not home. And always call your child's friend's parents to make sure they will be present and supervising if your child goes to a friend's house to hang out. While you can't have a GPS device implanted in your teenager, finding ways to keep track of where they are and who they're with will greatly reduce the likelihood that your children will use alcohol and other drugs.

PARTIES AND HANGING OUT
AT FRIENDS' HOMES

If your teen has a party at your house, even a small one, be there, not upstairs, not in another part of the house—pop in and out of the party. Take action to prohibit substance use—check on the kids, talk to them.

If your child is going to a party at a friend's house, investigate. Call the friend's parents to see if they'll be home during the party. Ask what they're doing to prevent drinking and other drug use during the party. Check in with your child occasionally to make sure she is okay and where you expect her to be. If the parents are not going to be home, you should not let your child go to the party.

Why all this concern? Because drugs and alcohol are a big part of the high school teen party scene. At parties where parents are not present, alcohol is sixteen times likelier to be available and marijuana is twenty-nine times likelier to be available.

Most parents don't realize that these substances are available at the parties their teens attend. One-third of teen partygoers report that parents are rarely or never present at the parties they attend.

The presence of parents can reduce the likelihood that alcohol and other drugs will be available, but it does not guarantee a substance-free party. While almost all parents say that they would not serve alcohol to teen partygoers in their homes, one-third of teen partygoers

---

Early on, I talked to parents who assured me they were chaperoning their children's parties. When I found out, on more than one occasion, that a parent's word could not necessarily be relied on, I put the onus on our children: No staying at homes without parental supervision.

Parent posting on CASA Parent Power discussion forum

A senior girl spoke of attending a New Year's party where more than one hundred high school kids showed up, drank heavily, and tore the place apart right in front of the father of the house. "It was freaky," she says. "I didn't have any respect for him. He was in the room the whole time, and he just let it all happen. I would never allow that kind of party in my house. He's supposed to be the parent."

Marc Fisher, "Are You a Toxic Parent?"
Washington Post Magazine, July 30, 2006

say they have attended parties where teens were drinking alcohol, smoking pot, or using cocaine, ecstasy, or prescription drugs *while a parent was present*; nearly half of seventeen-year-olds have attended such parties.

How can you be sure your child isn't drinking or drugging while at a friend's home? As Ronald Reagan said, "Trust, but verify." Speak with your kids about your expectations for their behavior both in your own home and in the homes of others. Call the parents of your child's friend and ask whether alcohol (or other drugs) will be available. Ask the parents what precautions they are taking to ensure the safety of all the kids at the party. While you cannot (and should not) police your child's every action inside and outside your home, you should maintain family rules and expectations about behavior.

MOVING TOWARD SENIOR YEAR

Getting older—moving to the later teen years—increases the chances that your son or daughter will smoke, drink, or use drugs. Why? Because each year these substances will become more available to them. Two-thirds of sixteen- and seventeen-year-olds can buy marijuana in

I was venting to one of my guy friends about studying, and
he turned to me and said, "Want me to give you some
Adderall? I'll give you a good deal for four or five of them."
I just stared at him. I never realized people would take
Adderall to cheat like that!

Seventeen-year-old student, "Pill Swapping,"
Teen Vogue, November 2007

a day or less; only 11 percent of twelve-year-olds can do so. Almost
half of seventeen-year-olds have friends who abuse prescription drugs;
only 10 percent of twelve-year-olds do.

In the later teens, your children will see more of their "cool" or
popular classmates, teammates, or friends experimenting with drugs,
with little or no apparent harm, oblivious to the danger to their developing brains. Your children will start dating, and pushing the en-
velope of "adulthood," increasing their independence and mobility.
By the time they turn seventeen, your children will almost certainly

**Percentage of Teens with Friends Who Abuse
Prescription Drugs**

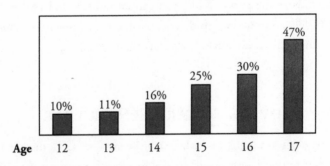

CASA. *National Survey of American Attitudes on Substance
Abuse XIII: Teens and Parents (2008)*

be offered drugs like alcohol, marijuana, acid, Adderall, Ritalin, and other pills, and perhaps cocaine and heroin, and they will likely know friends and classmates who use such drugs. At seventeen, many, perhaps most, of your children's friends will drink, at least occasionally.

You cannot shield them from every risk. But by being aware of the shifting dangers and opportunities in their lives, you can take extra care in the later teen years to reinforce the groundwork of communication and no-use messages you began to establish when your children were younger.

ENTERING COLLEGE

The freshman year of college (notably during the first semester) marks the biggest increase in smoking, drinking, and marijuana use among young Americans. It is a time of unprecedented freedom from supervision, rampant binge drinking among classmates, and easy availability not only of alcohol and marijuana but of just about every illegal and prescription drug. This time is so critical for your sons and daughters that I have devoted Chapter 13, "How Can I Prepare My Kids for College?" to the use of your Parent Power to get your children ready for college and through those years.

THE INFLUENCE OF FRIENDS

Social interactions and peer influence can contribute to drug use. Having friends who smoke is one of the main reasons that teens start smoking.

Teens say that one of the pressures they feel to begin using drugs is because their friends do, with curiosity as a close runner-up. After curiosity, a commonly cited explanation for initial drug use is "to be cool." Older teens appear more susceptible to such peer influences.

Drug-using friends may encourage or prompt your teen to experiment. If your son is drinking at a party, a friend who smokes pot may suggest that he should try marijuana because "It gives you a better buzz than beer, and faster, with no hangover." Another friend may tell your teen a story about how she tried OxyContin and how it was an amazing experience, arousing your teen's curiosity to try it too. A friend who smokes meth may claim that it helps her to study for exams; at the end of the following semester your son may try Ritalin or Adderall, hoping that it will help him concentrate and improve his grades. Your daughter's friends may decide that they are all going to take ecstasy together at the prom, and offer your daughter a pill in the car. This kind of peer pressure is frequently associated with drug initiation among teens.

Becoming part of a social group that uses can lead your teen to drink and experiment with drugs. So get to know your children's friends. Create opportunities to spend time with them. Invite them over for dinner or offer to drive them to activities. Ask your children about their friends, what they enjoy, and whether anyone in their circle is drinking, smoking cigarettes or pot, or abusing prescription drugs. These conversations can create opportunities to help your child navigate the teen social scene and to reinforce rules and values.

To the extent possible, become acquainted with your children's friends' families too. Simply calling the parents and speaking to them to confirm that your children are together and safe will go a long way in establishing communication about what's going on with your kids.

If possible, make your house the "fun" place for your children and their friends to hang out. Create a recreation room or other space in your home where the kids feel comfortable. Check in on them occasionally—bring them a snack, offer to order them a pizza, or take them to the movies. You will be surprised by how much you can be there, even when your children are with their friends.

BALANCING THE INFLUENCE OF FRIENDS

Parents often wonder how they can balance out the influence of their children's friends. The answer is by being an engaged parent. If you have a good relationship with your children, and are able to talk to them openly about alcohol and other drug use, they are much more likely to emulate your values and expectations, rather than those of their friends. One of the most common reasons that kids give for abstaining from drugs is that they don't want to disappoint their parents. Your children really do care about what you think of them— even more than they care about what their friends think.

ROMANTIC RELATIONSHIPS

Teenagers spend a great deal of time with their friends, and sometimes even more time with their crushes. These relationships can be healthy and productive and an important part of growing up. However, you should be aware of the connection between some aspects of teen dating and the risk of smoking, drinking, and using illegal drugs.

Teenagers fall in love. Indeed, psychiatrists say that for many people teenage love may be the most intense love experience of their lives. These intense relationships can be magical, but they can also be times of increased risk for your child.

Know if your teen is going out with a boyfriend or girlfriend, who this person is, and how much time your teen spends with that person. Teens who spend twenty-five or more hours per week with a boyfriend or girlfriend are almost five times likelier to get drunk and smoke marijuana than teens who spend less than ten hours per week with their girlfriend or boyfriend. While I don't know the reason for this statistical correlation, it may be that time spent with a significant other takes away from time spent with family or otherwise engaged in productive activities. In some cases, it may be that the significant other encourages your child to use. Or it may be that alcohol and drugs are seen as sexual disinhibitors. If your teen is spending a lot of time with a boyfriend or girlfriend, getting to know that person may help you determine whether your teen is one of those at higher risk.

Another factor is age. Teen girls whose boyfriends are two or more years older are much likelier to drink, get drunk, and smoke marijuana, compared to girls with boyfriends who are closer to their own age or girls who don't have boyfriends. Think about how dramatically different are the worlds of fourteen- and fifteen-year-old girls compared to the worlds of sixteen- and seventeen-year-old boys. Remember that two-thirds of sixteen- and seventeen-year-olds can buy marijuana in a day or less, compared with less than one-third of fourteen-year-olds. Alcohol and drugs are easily available in the world of the older boy; he's likely going to parties and other events, or hanging out with peers in places where such substances are common, or he may have a fake ID that he uses to buy beer. If your daughter is dating someone who is several years older, spend as much time as you can getting to know that person and assess his influence on your daughter. If you're concerned, consider ways to convince your daughter to end the relationship or limit the time and activities she spends with her beau.

Hopefully, you will have a close enough relationship with your teen to know whether your son or daughter is sexually active, or at least you will be a savvy enough parent to suspect when this is the case. It's important because sexually active teens are far more likely to get into alcohol and drugs. Some use such substances as sexual disinhibitors. The concern here for parents is not only drug or alcohol use. Most unplanned teenage pregnancies occur when one or both of the participants are high at the time of conception. The combined risk of substances and sex is so important for you and your child to understand that I've dedicated Chapter 10, "What's the Relationship Between Alcohol, Drugs, and Sexual Activity?" to this subject.

PARENT TIPS

- Reinforce parental messages and ask more questions about substance use during the transition times.
- Be present when children are socializing in your home.
- When your child goes to a party, ask the hosting parents what they are doing to make sure that drugs and alcohol won't be available.
- Don't let your children attend parties where adults are not present or where alcohol or drugs are.
- After school, make sure your child is supervised, especially when hanging out with friends, and engaged in extracurricular activities.
- Know who your child's friends are and who your child is dating. Create opportunities to speak to or get acquainted with their parents as well.
- Make your home the fun place for the kids to hang out.

7

IN WHAT CIRCUMSTANCES IS MY CHILD AT INCREASED RISK OF DRUG USE?

How you deal with the characteristics and situations that increase your child's risk of substance abuse should be tailored to your family's values and your child's specific circumstances and needs. But as soon as you suspect that your child is struggling with a serious behavioral, mental, emotional, drug, or alcohol problem, seek professional help.

FAMILY DISRUPTIONS AND TRAUMA: DIVORCE, FREQUENT MOVES, DEATH OF A LOVED ONE, CHILD ABUSE

Family disruptions—everything from a separation or divorce, to a death in the family, to frequent geographic moves and traumas such as physical or sexual abuse—cause significant stress and anxiety in a teenager and can strain the relationship between you and your child.

During these disruptions your child is more susceptible to the lure of alcohol, tobacco, and drugs.

Divorce

Parental divorce can have a devastating impact on a child and sharply spike the risk for substance use. Teens with divorced parents are much likelier to drink alcohol and use drugs than those whose parents are not divorced. This increase in risk occurs, in some cases, immediately upon learning of the divorce. But even for very young children, the emotional trauma of their parents' divorce is cumulative and the risk of substance abuse may increase over time.

Children of divorced parents confront a change in lifestyle, often including lots more—or lots less—money, a move to a new school or home, and inconsistent support and attention from Mom and Dad. These stressful circumstances can lead children to smoke, drink, and use drugs.

Sometimes divorce means that the child spends more or all of their time with one parent. The loss of a positive relationship with both Mom and Dad is disturbing to children, so it is important that divorced or separated spouses make arrangements that permit both parents to maintain a good relationship with their children. It's critical that both parents agree to send the same messages about alcohol and drugs to their children. Teens who continue to have a good relationship with both parents and get such messages are less susceptible to engaging in risky behaviors such as substance abuse.

Moving Frequently

Moving and changing schools frequently increases teens' risk of substance abuse. Teens, especially girls, who move frequently (six or more times in a five-year period) from one neighborhood or home to another and change schools in the process are at high risk of smoking, drinking, and using marijuana. Children whose home lives are unstable due to frequent relocations are more likely to suffer from behavioral, emotional, and academic problems, all of which hike the risk for substance abuse.

Frequent moves are often associated with economic hardship (e.g., parents can't afford to stay in their home) or new family configurations (moving in with a parent's new spouse), which are stressful for children. In addition, parents who move frequently tend to have weaker ties in their community and are able to invest less time and money in supporting and supervising their children. Children who are uprooted frequently may resent their parents, or otherwise have poorer relationships with their parents. Being the new kid in the class may make it likelier to be befriended by more deviant youngsters who may be more inclined to use drugs, and the new kid in the class may be tempted to do so to get accepted by that group. All of these factors can increase a child's susceptibility to peer pressure and risk of drinking and drug use.

Death, Disability, or Illness in the Family

A death, serious illness, or disability of a family member can be profoundly stressful for children. The loss of a parent or primary caretaker is traumatic not only for the child, but also for other surviving family members. Prolonged grief can negatively affect family cohesion and parental engagement. A serious illness or disability can disrupt normal family routines. The healthy family members may need to take on additional responsibilities, or forgo certain activities, to accommodate the sick family member. High health-care costs can create an economic hardship that negatively affects the family's lifestyle.

Traumatic Incidents

God forbid, if you learn your child is the victim of sexual or physical abuse, promptly seek professional help so that you and your child can deal with this awful situation and its dangerous consequences. Children who are subjected to incidents of such abuse are at high risk of self-medicating their pain by abusing alcohol and prescription and illegal drugs. So too are children who witness acts of domestic violence between their mother and father.

SOCIAL, DEVELOPMENTAL, BEHAVIORAL, AND MENTAL HEALTH PROBLEMS

Just about every teen will experience teenage angst; it's part of growing up. Parents need to know their kids well enough to distinguish serious emotional and behavioral issues from the normal mood swings, rebellious behavior, and boundary pushing that marks teenage development. This can sometimes be difficult; when in doubt, don't hesitate to seek professional help.

Social, developmental, behavioral, and mental health problems hike the risk of substance abuse for teens—and substance abuse in turn can intensify these problems. Adolescents with social anxiety, eating disorders, learning disabilities, attention deficit/hyperactivity disorder, or depression may struggle more than others to thrive, to excel, and even just to fit in. These teens often use substances to help them cope, self-medicate, or escape the stress of their everyday lives.

Struggling with a social, developmental, mental health, or behavioral problem does not mean that your child will drink or do drugs, only that there is a greater risk of doing so. If you see signs that your child is experiencing any of these problems, you should address it promptly by seeking professional help. But your job does not end there. Stay engaged in your child's life and monitor progress. Talk to your child honestly about the lures and dangers of smoking, drinking, and drugs. And be on guard for symptoms of substance abuse. In Chapter 14, "The Signs of Use—What to Do If You See Them," I describe the warning signals of smoking, drinking, and illegal and prescription drug abuse that you should look out for.

Kids who use substances, especially at young ages, often have some underlying emotional or mental health problem as well. The research at CASA, and the work of many experts in substance abuse and mental illness, have revealed that kids who smoke cigarettes at young ages may be experiencing depression or anxiety, or some other emotional or psychological problem. High school girls who smoke or drink are nearly twice as likely as those who don't to be depressed. Teens who smoke marijuana or pop pills, or who frequently abuse alcohol, are more likely than those who don't to be suffering from emotional or psychological ailments. Early and frequent use of marijuana increases the risk of a psychotic illness. And the odds are that those who get into drugs like methamphetamine, cocaine, and heroin have some co-occurring mental illness.

In these circumstances, it is not sufficient simply to say, "Stop smoking" or "Stop drinking" or "Stop using." A child who is self-medicating will need your help—and that of a pediatrician, psychologist, or psychiatrist—in order to deal with the related underlying emotional or psychological problems. You will not be able to treat the drug use, or even end the cigarette smoking, of such a tween or young teen without tackling the underlying problem.

Drug use has the potential to trigger certain mental illnesses in teens who have a genetic susceptibility (e.g., carry the DNA that contributes to such conditions). So, if there is a history of mental illness in your family, discuss it with your children when they're the appropriate age. Warn them about the added risk of substance use so that they can know how important it is for them to avoid it.

[At age twelve] I was diagnosed with depression. And at
the time, the medication they were giving me wasn't the
right one . . . it wasn't doing what it should do. So I found
alcohol through my mother's liquor cabinet and started
drinking alcohol to make me feel better. It made me feel
better, so I drank more and more. But when I wouldn't drink,
my depression seemed to get lower, I was sadder . . . it
seemed like every time I stopped drinking, it was worse.

Jamie Breden, person in recovery, at CASA's
Double Jeopardy Conference 2007

THE SIGNS OF DEPRESSION

Many teenagers struggle with depression, but most of them never receive treatment. This may be why so many depressed teens turn to
substances to self-medicate. Drugs and alcohol can temporarily relieve your child's symptoms and make your child feel better. But with
repeated resort to those substances, the benefits will disappear, the
symptoms will become worse, and addiction becomes likelier.

Signs of depression in teens are easily confused with normal teenage behavior changes and mood swings. In observing your child, if
you notice a severe intensity of any of the following symptoms, or a
combination of several of them, it may indicate that your child is suffering from depression.

- Sadness or hopelessness
- Irritability, anger, or hostility
- Tearfulness or frequent crying
- Withdrawal from friends and family
- Loss of interest in activities, inability to enjoy previously favored
  activities

- Unexplained changes in eating and sleeping habits (too much or too little)
- Restlessness and agitation
- Feelings of worthlessness and guilt
- Lack of enthusiasm and motivation
- Fatigue or lack of energy
- Difficulty concentrating
- Frequent complaints of physical illness, such as headaches or stomachaches
- Talk of death or suicide

If you observe any of these symptoms, talk to your child about what is causing them. These symptoms could be either the cause or result of substance abuse or addiction. If you believe that your child is depressed, or abusing drugs or alcohol, or if the symptoms do not seem to be improving, seek professional help.

For more information about the symptoms and potential treatments for the various social, developmental, behavioral, and mental health problems that are common in adolescents, visit the American Academy of Child and Adolescent Psychiatry (AACAP) website at www.aacap.org or the Substance Abuse and Mental Health Services Administration, National Mental Health Information Center website at mentalhealth.samhsa.gov.

EATING DISORDERS

Children and teens with eating disorders are likelier to smoke and abuse alcohol and illicit drugs. While such disorders are far more common in younger girls, they can also be found in boys. Young girls suffering from anorexia may see tobacco, cocaine, methamphetamine, and even heroin as appetite suppressants. Bulimics may abuse alcohol, or self-medicate themselves with it, then purge themselves to avoid the calories. The mental distress that often accompanies eating disorders, such as anxiety and depression, increases the risk of self-medication with tobacco, alcohol, and illegal and prescription drugs.

LEARNING DISABILITIES

Learning disabilities are conditions of the brain that affect a child's ability to take in, process, or express information. They are not mental defects or impairments, and should not be confused with handicaps such as mental retardation or autism. There are four basic types of learning disabilities: reading disorders, mathematics disorders, disorders of written expression, and learning disorders not otherwise specified.

Children with learning disabilities are susceptible to the kinds of problems that precipitate drug and alcohol abuse—low self-esteem, academic difficulty, loneliness, and depression. Their anxious search for social acceptance tends to make these children easy targets for friends and classmates offering tobacco, alcohol, pills, marijuana, and other illegal drugs to be happy, get high, and be one of the cool kids.

The teenage years are a troubling time for many with learning disabilities (LD) and attention deficit/hyperactivity disorder (ADHD), when low self-esteem and academic failure are at their most pronounced, and the desire for social acceptance can lead to the use, abuse, and sometimes sale of drugs and alcohol.

Anne Ford, *On Their Own: Creating an Independent Future for Your Adult Child with Learning Disabilities and ADHD* (2007)

When she learned she had a learning disability, Carrick Forbes lost hope that she would ever be smart. Carrick numbed her pain and frustration with drugs: "I had felt stupid since I was five. Because to me, learning disabled meant nothing different than being mentally retarded. . . . I think that I just sort of tried to accept the fact that I was not smart. And I would never be very smart. And so that school was not my forte. And I should go try to find other outlets."

Interview with Ann Curry on *Dateline*, July 31, 2005

Identifying learning disabilities early on and attending to the special needs of children with them can provide the support these children need to overcome their emotional issues and to help them steer clear of alcohol and other drugs.

BEHAVIORAL DISORDERS AND CONDUCT PROBLEMS

Some children have difficulty sitting still, following rules, or behaving in a socially acceptable way. They act out, rebel, argue, talk back, resist authority, and get into trouble frequently. Such children may have a behavioral disorder.

Behavioral disorders include attention deficit/hyperactivity disorder (ADHD), conduct disorder (CD), and oppositional defiant disorder (ODD). ADHD generally involves an unwillingness or inability to sit still, be quiet, pay attention, or focus. Symptoms of ADHD include inattention, hyperactivity, and/or impulsivity. If your child shows symptoms of ADHD, you should seek professional advice. If not properly treated, ADHD raises the risk of smoking, drinking, and drug use.

Conduct disorder involves more outwardly destructive behaviors such as lying, stealing, damaging property, fighting, or aggression toward others. Children with this disorder have a hard time following rules and behaving in a socially acceptable way.

Children are naturally defiant from time to time; they may argue, talk back, and disobey their parents or teachers. But a small percentage of children are consistently defiant, to the extent that it can interfere with their social, academic, and family life. Oppositional defiant disorder is defined as an ongoing pattern of uncooperative, defiant, and hostile behavior toward parents, teachers, and other authority figures that seriously interferes with the youngster's day-to-day functioning. Symptoms include constant temper tantrums, excessive arguing, active defiance, frequent anger and resentment, deliberate attempts to annoy, upset, or even hurt people, and revenge seeking.

If your child is exhibiting conduct problems, it signals risk of a host of future problems, including substance abuse. For teens with conduct problems, drug use may become another way of acting out. More boys tend to exhibit conduct problems than girls, but girls who display them are even more likely than boys to abuse drugs and alcohol.

If your teen is regularly disobeying rules, lying, stealing, fighting, being kicked out of class, sent to the principal's office, or caught breaking the rules, you should seek professional help. Your child may be struggling with some coexisting or underlying mental health problems that can be treated.

STRESS, BOREDOM, SPENDING MONEY

Our research has taught us that certain aspects of a teen's lifestyle may increase the chances of using drugs. For instance, high stress, frequent boredom, and too much spending money can be a dangerous combination for any American teen. Teens who share two or more of these characteristics are three times likelier to smoke, drink, and use illegal drugs.

Stress

A quarter of teens say they feel a great deal of stress in their day-to-day lives. These high-stress teens are twice as likely to smoke, drink, get drunk, and use illegal drugs. Stress in a teenager's life can be caused by a variety of factors, such as living conditions (poverty, homelessness, an abusive home environment) or typical teenage experiences (schoolwork, dating, making friends, being rejected by classmates). Teens who are stressed-out may turn to drugs to seek relief from their anxiety or to forget their troubles.

As the following chart illustrates, teens experiencing high stress are more likely to report having used tobacco, alcohol, and marijuana.

If your child is stressed-out, look for the reasons why. If it's too

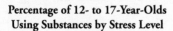

**Percentage of 12- to 17-Year-Olds
Using Substances by Stress Level**

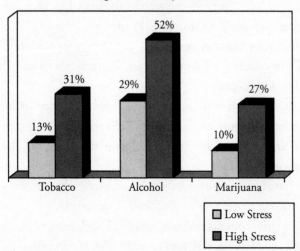

*CASA. National Survey of American Attitudes on Substance
Abuse VIII: Teens and Parents (2003)*

much school work or too many extracurricular activities, talk to the school and your child about making adjustments in the schedule. If there's tension because of economic problems in the family, or the death of a close relative, spend the time with your child to explain that these are all part of the experience of life that everyone may face. If there's a serious illness in the family, suggest things that your child can do—"Why don't you call Grandma? That'll make her feel better," or "Say a prayer for Grandpa." If the tension is from being rejected by friends, not invited to a party, or breaking up with a girlfriend or boyfriend, tell your child about similar situations that you went through when you were a teen and how you moved on and learned from that experience. Use your Parent Power to put things in perspective for your daughter or son.

Boredom

How often have you heard your child say, "I'm bored" or, "This is soooo boring."

Boredom is a common complaint of teens when they are doing something they don't want to do: "Homework is boring," "Straightening up my room is boring," "Cleaning the dishes is boring." That kind of boredom is typical of teens, and every mother and father has heard their kids express it.

But nearly a fifth of teens in a CASA survey said they are bored all the time, or frequently bored by almost everything. If your teen is one of those, be careful. Such teens are likelier to use drugs and alcohol to relieve their boredom.

Compared to teens who are not bored, teens who are often bored are more likely to use tobacco, alcohol, or marijuana.

If your child complains about constant boredom, get him involved in solving the problem. Ask him to make a list of fun things he'd like to do, then help him do those things. In addition to inspiring him to

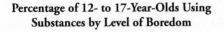

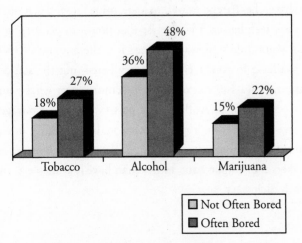

**Percentage of 12- to 17-Year-Olds Using
Substances by Level of Boredom**

CASA. *National Survey of American Attitudes on Substance
Abuse VIII: Teens and Parents (2003)*

get involved in activities that interest him, this will encourage development of self-reliance and problem-solving skills.

Spending Money

Giving your children more money than they need, or allowing them to earn and spend significant amounts of their own money, may enable them to buy cigarettes, alcohol, and other drugs. The more money a teen has to spend in a week, the likelier that teen is to smoke, drink and use marijuana. A CASA survey of twelve- to seventeen-year-olds in 2003 found that teens who had more than fifty dollars in weekly spending money were more than twice as likely to try cigarettes, alcohol, and marijuana, compared to kids who had fifteen dollars or less to spend per week. Girls who had a lot of spending money—more than fifty dollars a week—were even more likely to smoke, drink, and use drugs than boys with the same weekly allowance.

You have the Parent Power to determine how much spending money your teen has each week. Use that power to place appropriate limits on your child's allowance. Since it is the amount of spending money available to your teen that is key here—not the source—it's also important for you to exercise some control over what your teen does with money made working at a part-time job. Encourage your teen to save some of it for a special occasion, like a concert or a major sports event, or for some trendy clothing, electronic devices, or expensive sneakers they might want, rather than have it available as free-to-spend cash each week.

PARENT TIPS

- Seek professional advice if your child exhibits symptoms of an eating disorder, learning disability, conduct disorder, attention deficit/hyperactivity disorder, oppositional defiant disorder, or depression.
- After a divorce or separation, ensure that both parents remain engaged in your child's life and send consistent messages about substance use.
- If you move frequently, find ways to create stability and to maintain relationships that are important to your child.
- Reinforce family cohesion after a death, disability, or serious illness in the family.
- Encourage your child to overcome boredom by getting involved in after-school activities, learning new skills, or finding other means of entertainment.
- Make sure your child doesn't have too much spending money.
- Get professional help if your child is the victim of or witness to a traumatic event like domestic violence.

8

HOW CAN I MAKE MY HOME A SAFE HAVEN?

Families have the greatest influence on children—for better or worse. For parents who want to raise drug-free children, looking in the mirror is the crucial first step.

You have the Parent Power to instill positive, healthy attitudes in your children, and this goes hand in hand with your responsibility to create a healthy environment for your children to grow up in. If you smoke, drink excessively, abuse prescription drugs, or use illegal drugs, it is important to stop. If you need help doing so, then get help fast: for your own sake and for the sake of your children.

Parents are the number one influence, but they aren't the only ones in the family whose behavior children mimic. Other close relatives—siblings, cousins, uncles, and even close family friends—can have a significant impact on your child's propensity to use tobacco, alcohol, or illegal drugs.

Older relatives can serve as loyal protectors, their conduct can set a good example, and they can provide a support system that helps children to stay substance free.

Several of Robert and Ethel Kennedy's children developed serious substance abuse problems. One of their close family friends was reported to have been a heroin addict and facilitated the children's use. Their son David Kennedy struggled with heroin addiction and died in 1984 of a drug overdose. David's brother Robert F. Kennedy, Jr., also struggled with heroin addiction but eventually overcame it.

Family members in recovery from addiction to alcohol or drugs who share their insights and struggles with your children can be a healthy and powerful positive influence. But a relative or friend of yours who uses can be a bad influence on your child. Your children may want to be cool and get high like their older cousin or big brother or aunt. Older relatives who smoke, drink, or use drugs may offer these substances to younger relatives, or otherwise encourage your children to use them.

BEWARE OF BIG BROTHERS AND SISTERS WHO USE

When an older brother or sister is using drugs or drinking heavily it puts the younger siblings at high risk. These younger siblings are twice as likely to smoke, drink, or use illegal drugs as the average teen. Even if the younger sibling merely thinks that the older brother or sister is using—regardless of the truth—the younger sibling is still at greater risk of substance abuse than the average teen.

In CASA surveys, more than one in ten teens said an older brother or sister encouraged them to use illegal drugs and even offered them such drugs. Such a sibling is a "pusher" in the family, who increases the risk that your child will use.

We would have weekly sleepovers and several of the kids I hung out with had older brothers or older sisters in high school that were experimenting with drugs. So I remember my first experience was a kid that had stolen marijuana from his brother and brought it to the house and we all tried it.

Vincent Lobell, recovering drug user and substance abuse counselor at Outreach House in Brentwood, NY, speaking at CASA's Family Matters conference, 2004

When children grow up with a sibling who abuses or is addicted to alcohol or other drugs, the sober sibling suffers as well. Parents (understandably) may spend lots of energy and time to help the child with the substance abuse problem, and give less attention to their other children. Sober siblings may feel left out, angry, or ashamed that their family is different. If you are a parent in such a situation, be sensitive to what your sober child is feeling; talk openly about what is going on in the family, educate him about the other sibling's disease, and explain why you need to spend so much time working with the other sibling's illness.

If the sober sibling is struggling to cope with his own feelings, reach out to support groups for family members of addicts, such as Al-Anon, for help. It may be natural for the sober sibling to adopt the role of the good child or the responsible child in response to the other sibling's illness. Realize that even "positive" roles such as these can be difficult to live up to, and may create additional stress for the sober child. Last, your sober child will also feel pain, so make sure that child knows how much you love him, and that you would do the same for him if he got sick with a terrible disease.

Family members do not operate in a vacuum—the behavior of each family member impacts the entire unit, for good and for ill.

If any of your children's relatives are smokers, use drugs, or have a drinking problem, ask them to set a good example for your child by not using around your child and by encouraging your child not to use. This may also be an opportunity to talk with your child about the relative and the consequences of the relative's use.

You don't have to have a perfect family to set a good example for your child. Let's be real, does anyone have a perfect family? But if you strive to set a healthy example, and encourage older siblings and other relatives to do the same, your children will adopt your family's healthy attitudes about drinking, smoking, and other drug use.

FAMILY CONTRACTS

Some families choose to put rules about tobacco, alcohol, and other drug use in writing, in the form of a "family contract." The benefit of a family contract is that it forces everyone to discuss what parents' expectations of their children's behavior are, and ensures that the rules and consequences are clear and understood by all.

It's best to concentrate on a plan for your family if your child does decide to abuse alcohol or other drugs. Lots of teens will [try] alcohol and/or other drugs before they graduate high school. Let everyone know what the plan is before it becomes an issue.

This way there are no surprises.

A written and signed contract with the consequences spelled out will do more than anything else. Trust me, I know!!!

Parent posting on CASA Parent Power discussion forum

Parents can also agree to certain obligations, like providing a safe ride home, that encourage the children to uphold their commitment to leave parties where alcohol and other drugs are available. Signing a contract together may also increase the likelihood that children will abide by the rules. Here's an example of what a family contract might look like, to help you draft your own.

Sample Household Contract

Child   I, (name of child), agree this is a tobacco- and drug-free household, and that alcohol will be used only in moderation by adults. I agree to refrain from using any substances inside or outside our home.

Parent(s) I(we), (name of parents), agree this is a tobacco- and drug-free household. I(we) know that smoking and abusing alcohol or prescription drugs, or using illicit drugs, may put my(our) child at risk and agree to set the right example regarding substance use both inside and outside our home.

Our family agrees on the following substance-use rules:

- Young people will not drink alcohol, smoke cigarettes, or use any drugs.
- Young people will not stay at parties where alcohol or other drugs are available. The consequence of doing so will be _____.
- Young people will not drive drunk or high, or accept a ride in a car with a driver who has been drinking. Doing so will result in a punishment of _____.

- Parents agree to pick up kids at any time if they need a safe ride home.
- Young people will not allow their guests to bring alcohol, drugs, or cigarettes into our house.
- No one, including parents, is to make alcohol available to anyone under age twenty-one.
- Older brothers and sisters will encourage younger brothers and sisters to not drink, smoke, or use drugs.

We agree to abide by these rules, to treat one another with mutual respect, and to keep the channels of communication open.

_____   _____

Child   Date

_____   _____

Parent(s)   Date

You can find another sample contract at Family.SAMHSA.gov/media/familyguide/pdfs/alcohol-contract.pdf.

DISCUSS YOUR FAMILY'S HISTORY OF ADDICTION

Many families have at least one member who has struggled with the disease of addiction. Perhaps you have a grandfather who drank heavily every night, an uncle who never grew out of smoking pot every

Alcoholism devastated the Barrymore family. Patriarch
John Barrymore was a great actor whose career was
ruined by his drinking. His son, John Jr., followed in his
father's footsteps; his acting career also collapsed due to
his drug and alcohol use. John Jr.'s daughter, Drew, has
been struggling to escape the same fate; she entered rehab
at the age of thirteen, after drinking alcohol at the age of
nine, smoking pot at the age of ten, and taking cocaine at
the age of twelve.

day, a grandmother who died of lung cancer or emphysema because
she didn't quit smoking, or an elderly aunt who constantly pops tranquilizers, to the family's great amusement or alarm. If you're not sure
about your own family history, ask some relatives, do a little investigating. If there is anyone in your family who has struggled with
addiction, your child may be at increased risk of substance abuse and
addiction.

We now understand that genetic as well as environmental factors
can play a large role in the transmission of tobacco, alcohol, and drug
addiction from one generation to the next. Parents, family, friends,
and the community all influence whether a child decides to experiment with substances. However, once a child has begun to smoke,
drink, or use drugs, genetic factors can influence, perhaps determine,
whether that child's use will descend into abuse or addiction. Similarly, the ability to tolerate a substance without becoming impaired
may be strongly influenced by genetic makeup, which in turn may
increase your child's tendency to abuse that substance.

Too often families overlook or conceal their own history of substance abuse and fail to warn the next generation. One big reason is
shame, which stems from the stigma attached to the disease of addiction. Another reason is that addiction was not always viewed the same

way in prior generations. The lecherous uncle who always got drunk and hit on the waitress at family functions may not have been labeled an alcoholic, even if that is, in fact, what he was. Another mistake that families make is thinking that addictions to various substances are not related. But the same genetic predisposition that influenced one family member to drink too much may lead another to become addicted to marijuana, cocaine, or even heroin.

If there is any history of addiction in your family it may increase the risk that your children develop a substance-abuse problem. When you talk to your children about not smoking, drinking, or using drugs, tell them about this family risk, that addiction is a disease and that it has a genetic component. Another time you might feel comfortable discussing such a family matter is during your child's pediatric exam: "Doctor, I have something to share with you and my son about our family's medical history."

You and your children should not feel somehow doomed or marked by such a family history. As with any other disease that is linked to genetics—cancer, heart disease, diabetes—environment and lifestyle factors play a role in whether your child will develop the disease of addiction. If diabetes runs in your family, your children can learn to monitor their sugar intake and watch their weight. If certain types of cancer run in your family, your children can learn to watch their diet and get screenings at an earlier age. So it is with addiction. If this disease runs in your family, your children can choose, for example, not to drink—and you should be vigilant to watch for the signs and symptoms of substance abuse I describe in Chapter 14.

It's important to understand that . . . because you are prone
to addiction doesn't mean that you're going to become
addicted. It just says that you've got to be careful.

Glen Hanson, DDS, PhD; professor, University
of Utah; director, Utah Addiction Center; former
director of The National Institute on Drug Abuse

PRENATAL EXPOSURE TO TOBACCO, ALCOHOL, AND OTHER DRUGS INCREASES THE LIKELIHOOD OF FUTURE DRUG USE

Children exposed to tobacco, alcohol, and other drugs in the womb
are at risk for developing physical, mental, and cognitive disorders.
The resulting problems that these children face often continue into
adolescence and adulthood, increasing the likelihood of alcohol and
other drug abuse.

Of all the substances of abuse—including cocaine, heroin, and
marijuana—studies show that alcohol causes the most damage to the
brain of a developing fetus. Children with fetal alcohol syndrome
(FAS) and fetal alcohol spectrum disorders (FASD)—which occur
in the children of mothers who drank alcohol while pregnant—
suffer behavioral problems such as hyperactivity and attention defi-
cits, memory difficulties, poor problem-solving and arithmetic skills,
lower IQ scores, and troubles with language, perception, and motor
development. These problems render the child susceptible to substance abuse.

Even moderate levels of prenatal exposure to alcohol can have det-
rimental effects on behavior and diminish a child's ability to learn.
Prenatal exposure to alcohol is associated with antisocial and delin-
quent conduct during adolescence and young adulthood, including

poor impulse control and social adaptation, aggressive sexual behavior, trouble with the law, problems holding a job, and alcohol and drug abuse and addiction.

Children exposed to tobacco in the womb may suffer a variety of long-term consequences, including lower IQ, deficiencies in verbal, reading, and math skills, and an increased risk for conduct disorders, attention deficit/hyperactivity disorder, and related alcohol and other drug dependence.

Marijuana exposure in the womb can slow a baby's growth and affect a child's IQ, reasoning ability, memory, and academic performance. It can also lead to mental illness, such as depression, anxiety, and behavioral problems such as inattention and impulsivity. Children prenatally exposed to marijuana may be more vulnerable to the addictive power of marijuana and other drugs, including OxyContin and heroin.

Cocaine exposure in the womb similarly affects a child's attention and alertness, IQ, and motor skills. School-age children exposed to cocaine in the womb display subtle but discernible differences in their ability to plan and problem-solve. Such children may have to work harder—and need more help to focus their attention, remain alert, and process information. Heroin and other opiate exposure in the womb similarly affects children.

If you have a child who was exposed prenatally to nicotine, alcohol, or other drugs, be on the lookout for health and behavioral problems. Spotting these problems early and monitoring your child for the signs of substance abuse described in Chapter 14 will help your child grow up free of drug and alcohol abuse.

PROTECT CHILDREN FROM
ENVIRONMENTAL TOBACCO SMOKE

If you are a parent who is a smoker, give it up now—and not just for your own health. At the very least, make sure that you smoke outdoors, far away from your child. And never smoke in a car with your child—it's illegal in some states, and anywhere you do it, it's bad for your child's health.

Exposure to secondhand tobacco smoke has both short- and long-term effects on children. Children who are exposed to secondhand smoke are more likely to be admitted to the hospital and to develop a range of serious infections, including meningitis. Because the respiratory tract of a young child is not fully developed, children exposed to tobacco smoke are at greater risk for illnesses such as bronchitis, pneumonia, asthma, and sudden infant death syndrome (SIDS). For those children who develop asthma, secondhand smoke increases the frequency and severity of asthma attacks. Exposed children are more likely to suffer from ear infections and to have their tonsils and adenoids surgically removed. Exposure to secondhand smoke in the first few months of life appears to do the most harm.

The longer-term effects of secondhand smoke include higher risks of lung and other forms of cancer, atherosclerosis (hardening of the arteries), and coronary heart disease. Given the list and severity of harms caused by secondhand smoke, it's not surprising that former U.S. Surgeon General C. Everett Koop has called parents who smoke "child abusers."

If you need help to quit smoking, and many people do, there are lots of free smoking-cessation programs. Talk to your doctor or inquire whether your local health center, hospital, or your insurance plan offers such a program. The American Cancer Society website (www.cancer.org) can help you find a free, phone-based program, called a Quitline, in your community. The American Legacy Foundation offers a free online program, Ex, at www.becomeanex.org. Quit-Net at www.quitnet.com has helped many people stop smoking.

PARENT TIPS

- Set a good example for your child through your own behavior.
- Encourage relatives to do the same.
- If there is a history of addiction in your family, tell your children that they may have inherited a genetic propensity for the disease.
- If one of your children has a substance-abuse problem, reserve extra support and time for the sober sibling.
- If you are having trouble quitting drinking, smoking, or using drugs, get help.

9

WHAT YOU SHOULD KNOW ABOUT THE DIFFERENCES BETWEEN BOYS AND GIRLS

In America, your daughter or son can grow up to be anything: a doctor, nurse, lawyer, teacher, pilot, engineer, athlete, Wall Street banker, corporate CEO, senator, or president. Daughters and sons can both be at the top of their class, play the same sports with the same gusto, and socialize together on the same footing.

It should not be surprising then, that where smoking, drinking, and drugging are concerned, our daughters often act like Annie Oakley, belting out with cowgirl bravado: "Anything you can do, I can do better!" On the playing field and at the after-party, girls are keeping up. The docile daughters of days past, who were left behind when the boys went drinking, are a distant memory. Young women today hang with the guys and party with the girls. Unfortunately, this means that daughters are smoking cigarettes, drinking alcohol, and using drugs as much as sons.

This chart tells it all:

Smoking, Drinking, and Drug Use in High School (2007)

Percentage Who	High School Girls	High School Boys
Drink Alcohol	45%	45%
Binge Drink	24%	28%
Smoke Cigarettes	19%	21%
Use Marijuana	17%	22%
Tried Inhalants	14%	12%
Tried Steroids	3%	5%
Use Meth	4%	5%
Use Ecstasy	5%	7%
Use Cocaine	3%	4%
Tried Heroin	2%	3%

U.S. Department of Health & Human Services, Centers for Disease Control and Prevention, Youth Risk Behavior Surveillance System

The numbers above are low because they are based on what kids say about their own behavior, and we know that kids underreport their own substance use. But the boy-to-girl ratio of substance use is right on the mark. Girls are smoking, drinking, and using drugs at about the same rate as boys. Other surveys show that twelve- to seventeen-year-old girls are slightly more likely than boys to abuse prescription drugs, especially painkillers and tranquilizers.

Of course, each boy and girl is unique. But in the substance arena, you should be aware that girls share some common characteristics that differ from boys, and boys share some common characteristics that differ from girls. Boys and girls are wired differently.

While you should encourage your sons and daughters to achieve the same grades and pursue the same careers, when it comes to preventing substance abuse, understanding the differences between them is key to the effective use of your Parent Power. Here's what you need to know about the differences between sons and daughters:

1. Boys and girls often use substances for different reasons, exhibit use in different ways, respond to different risk factors, and suffer different consequences. Understanding this can help you to prevent your child's drinking or drug use, or to intervene early to stop it.

2. The manner and situations in which boys and girls are offered substances, and the people who offer substances to them, are likely to be different. Knowing this can help you prepare your child to resist offers to try cigarettes, alcohol, and other drugs.

3. The consequences of substance use for boys and girls vary. Girls can get addicted faster and may suffer the consequences of substance abuse more rapidly and severely than boys. Boys may suffer more injuries.

Understanding these differences will give you insights about how you talk to your sons and daughters about the risks and attraction of substances, how you answer their questions, and how you teach them to respond to the drug offers they receive.

Overall the message is the same. However, with the girls we've always stressed how vulnerable they become when under the influence.

For our son, we'll reinforce the bad-judgment message but also discuss the fact that violence often accompanies drugs and alcohol. We'll take him to an emergency room to hear, firsthand, from a nurse, about what she sees after midnight.

Parent posting on CASA Parent Power discussion forum

WHY TEENS USE DRUGS

By and large, teens use drugs for many of the same reasons that adults do. Sometimes teens take drugs because they're looking for a pleasurable experience; they want to feel something new and exciting. "I smoke weed because it makes everything more fun." Other times, teens turn to drugs to escape from negative feelings, such as anxiety, stress, unhappiness, or boredom. "I'm getting bad grades and I hate school. Getting high makes me feel better." Another reason teens use is social influence; teens may think it's cool, or want to fit in, or they may see people around them, even parents, doing it, and adopt their behavior. "Everyone drinks after the game, the guys would think I'm weird if I didn't."

While any teen caught drinking or using drugs may cite any of the reasons listed above, there often tend to be differences in the reasons why sons and daughters use drugs. Understanding these differences will help you identify potential risk factors in your own son or daughter. On the following pages I describe these differences in stark terms, but know that some boys will try drugs for reasons likelier for girls (e.g., peer pressure) and some girls will try them for reasons likelier for boys (e.g., sensation seeking).

BOYS WILL BE BOYS

Your son is more likely than your daughter to turn to addictive substances to satisfy his sensation-seeking impulses, show off, or be cool.

Sensation Seeking

What do I mean by sensation seeking? Scientists measure sensation seeking in terms of the extent to which someone seeks thrills and adventure, desires to have new experiences and cast off their inhibitions, or can't stand boredom. Sensation seeking is a perfectly normal impulse in teenagers, especially boys, but it can lead to trouble. It may prompt teenage boys to take dangerous risks, such as drag racing, driving while drunk, or using drugs.

If your son exhibits sensation-seeking behaviors, you probably wish you could tie him to a tree until he turns twenty-one. But you don't need to lock him up, just channel his impulses! You can reduce the likelihood that he will turn to drugs or other high-risk activities by encouraging him to take equally exciting, but safer, risks.

There are many activities that can satisfy your son's need for adventure and excitement, depending on his interests. He may enjoy rock climbing, skateboarding, dirt biking, taking trips (with you), doing outdoor activities such as survival training or being a scout leader, playing in a band, getting involved with social, political, or religious causes, or learning how to DJ. Sports, in particular, have been shown to have a protective effect against drug abuse (keep him away from performance-enhancing drugs like steroids). Another benefit of channeling sensation-seeking behavior is that you can build your son's confidence by getting him engaged in activities that develop life skills.

Showing Off and Being Cool

Boys are more prone to use drugs or drink to show off or be cool. The best defense here is helping your child develop critical-thinking skills and a strong sense of self. Ask your children if they would jump off a cliff to show off or be cool like some other guys, and they'd be quick to say, "No way!" That's probably because it's obvious to them that jumping off a cliff will kill you and is stupid.

Other activities, like having a few beers at a party, may not seem as obviously stupid, even to you. So how do you get your son to think twice before doing that? When it comes to steering themselves away from trying to be cool like other guys, your son needs to think critically about the activity. Smoking or drinking a few beers may feel good, but is it healthy for athletes to pollute their bodies like that? Try to help your son understand that when making important decisions, what really matters is what's best for him. What are his expectations for himself? Will drinking help him win the debate competition? Will he be able to ace his math test the next day? Is it worth losing his driving privileges? Teenage boys with good self-esteem, with a strong sense of who they are and what they want for their own lives, are less likely to drink and use drugs to appear cool.

GIRLS WILL BE GIRLS

Girls tend to use alcohol or drugs to improve their mood (i.e., to self-medicate), to increase their confidence, to reduce tension, to cope with problems, to lose their sexual and social inhibitions, or to be thin.

Self-medicating

Your daughter's low self-esteem, lack of confidence, depression, or anxiety are easily masked and may be overlooked. But there may be physical signs, and you can catch them if you're attentive. Pay attention to your daughter's sleeping habits; too much or too little sleep can be a symptom of a problem. Getting a sense of your daughter's self-confidence may require observing her interactions with others and listening to how she talks about herself. Or you can try a more direct approach and ask her questions about how she views herself or how she thinks others see her.

As a parent, you can help build your daughter's self-esteem and feelings of self-worth through encouragement and positive reinforcement. Good, old-fashioned love does wonders for children's self-esteem. Praise her, hug her, kiss her, and tell her she's great. Make sure she knows that you love her no matter what, even if she gets a bad grade, or talks back to you, or confesses that she got drunk. You can also help your daughter build her confidence and self-worth by getting her involved in activities such as sports, public speaking (e.g., debate team or teaching), community-service activities, an exciting job or internship, arts, drama, music, and taking care of others. (This can work for your son too.)

If your daughter is disappointed about a bad grade or not making a team, let her know that feeling disappointed is normal, and help her put the situation in perspective and refocus her energy in productive ways.

Finding constructive ways to work through and release negative feelings is a challenge that everyone faces at some point in their lives, but not one that everyone masters. Simply talking to your daughter or son about their feelings, and acknowledging that it's normal to have those feelings, can be helpful. Teaching your child healthy ways to cope with negative feelings will prepare your child to deal with the emotional crises that are sure to arise in life.

If you're worried that your daughter may suffer from depression or severe anxiety, you should seek professional help.

I was on a firm foundation [from my parents]. . . . If you fail, then you have to try to succeed. And you certainly can never be helped by liquor, and you never can be helped by dope. You just can't be.

Actress Katharine Hepburn, responding to Dick Cavett's question about how she survived the traps for young girls in Hollywood when so many others ended up tragically; *The Dick Cavett Show*, September 14, 1973

Dieting Dangers

Some girls today are literally killing themselves to be thin. Whether your daughter is simply dieting or engaging in more extreme measures of weight control, she is at greater risk for smoking, drinking, and using drugs.

Girls who are dieting may smoke and use drugs to suppress their appetites. Girls who engage in extreme dieting behaviors, such as not eating for twenty-four hours or more, taking diet pills, or bingeing and purging, drink more alcohol than those who don't engage in such behaviors. All girls who diet, even if they don't otherwise engage in unhealthy dieting behaviors, are likelier to smoke, and to smoke more cigarettes than those who don't diet. In extreme situations, girls may use methamphetamine or cocaine as appetitive suppressants.

If your daughter is taking extreme weight-control measures or is obsessed with being thin, she is likely being influenced by fashion magazines and pictures of ultrathin models. You can help her put the advertisements in *Vogue* and the pictures in *People* or *Us Weekly* in perspective. Talk to her about how unrealistic those figures and

Susan transferred to a new school in January. She was the new kid and had to make friends quickly and fit into the scene. Unfortunately, two things were very important in her new peer group. One was being thin and the other was doing everything possible to stay that way. So she became bulimic. Other than losing a little weight and feeling terrible, the experiment failed. In desperation, she resorted to cocaine. It took away her appetite and the pounds began shedding. However, her grades slipped and she became irritable. She lost the very friends she was trying to win over.

lifestyles are. Tell her about the history of "heroin chic" in the 1990s, where models took heroin to help project a washed out, toothpick-thin image in fashion magazines.

If your daughter is overweight, underweight, or overly concerned about her weight, be on the lookout for signs of substance use. Monitor her behavior for signs of bingeing or starvation—these can signal an eating disorder. You may need to make adjustments in your own behavior. For example, be careful about the comments you make. Encouraging overweight teens to diet may backfire and make matters worse. Here again, what you do will be far more persuasive than what you say. Modeling positive eating behavior can be more effective in changing your daughter's eating habits than verbal pressure to lose weight.

If your daughter is at an unhealthy weight (too much or too little), consider seeking the advice of a doctor or a nutritionist, or someone who specializes in eating disorders. Eating disorders require professional treatment.

Peer Influence

Though both are subject to peer pressure, your daughter is more likely than your son to go with the flow of the crowd. In fact, your daughter's peer group is one of the most important influences on whether she will smoke, drink, or use drugs. If she has friends who smoke, drink, or use drugs, she is more likely to do so herself, and the more friends she has who do these things, the more likely she is to do them too.

Understanding why your daughter may be influenced by her friends' behavior will enable you to use your Parent Power to help your daughter make her own decisions and stand by them, including a decision not to use substances.

Peer influence can work in many ways. Your daughter may respond to her peers' overt or perceived approval of smoking, drinking, or drug use. She may try to copy the substance-using behavior of her new role models—the popular girls at school. Sometimes, friends or classmates may pressure your daughter to try a cigarette, have a beer, or take a hit of marijuana.

When your daughter goes through puberty, she may start to compare herself (physically, socially, and academically) to her new peers. She may have doubts or insecurities about how she measures up. Perhaps as a means of coping with these insecurities and to fit in, your daughter may begin to model her own behavior after that of her peers. She may suppress her own thoughts, beliefs, and desires in favor of those of her peers, which makes her vulnerable to peer influence to smoke, drink, or use other drugs.

Your daughter is likely to spend a lot of time with her friends and to be involved in their lives. Her relationships with her friends are also likely to be very intimate and somewhat exclusive. She may look to friends, rather than family, for support when she is stressed out or in need of comfort. This dependence on her friends and her fear of rejection may cause your daughter to copy her friends' behaviors in order to cement the bond between them.

If your daughter is one of the popular girls, she is not immune to peer influence. Many popular girls feel that they are under more pressure to smoke and drink than other girls in order to maintain their image (sophisticated, independent).

You—Mom and Dad—can balance the influence of your child's peers by being engaged parents. Having a strong, positive relationship with your child will bolster her against peer pressure and reduce her risk of substance use. Having a strong bond with your daughter or son may also reduce the likelihood that they will maintain friendships with peers who smoke, drink, or use other drugs.

Sexual and Physical Abuse

As I said in Chapter 7, girls who are the victims of physical or sexual abuse—date rape, or an abusive relationship with a friend or family member—or who witness such abuse in their families are at high risk of resorting to alcohol and other drug use to self-medicate.

SAYING NO VS. SAYING YES

By this point, you are well aware that your child will be offered illegal drugs, alcohol, and tobacco before graduating from high school. Several factors distinguish the children who say yes from the children who say no. Although some of those factors may be out of your hands, the biggest factor is you!

Your children need to be prepared for that moment when the offer comes. Tweens and teens need to develop the will and skills to decline when they are offered cigarettes, alcohol, or illegal or prescription drugs. They want your help to do that. You can do role-playing exercises together, so your children can practice turning down an offer to drink, smoke, or take illegal drugs. Role-playing is a good way for your children to explore responding to different kinds of pressure, for example, "C'mon, all the cool kids are doing it," or "It will make you feel good." Also, you should take turns with your children, and have them try to pressure you into doing something dangerous too. This is a nice way for you to throw out some examples of responses that your children can use in real life, without sounding too preachy.

You may prefer to simply discuss the situations your children are likely to face. However you approach the subject, you will be most effective if you know the different circumstances under which boys and girls are commonly offered substances.

Coaching Boys to Turn Down Drug Offers

Your son is likelier to be offered drugs at an earlier age than your daughter.

The offer is likely to occur in a public place where boys hang out, such as a park, playground, or on the street. This means that it may be easier for your son to walk away from the situation when it happens—but it may be harder for your son to avoid places where drug offers occur.

Boys are more likely to be offered alcohol, marijuana, and other drugs by a male relative (e.g., an uncle, cousin, or older sibling), a male friend, or a male stranger. These men may be role models, or they may be intimidating to your son, depending on your son's relationship with them. The person offering is more likely to emphasize the "benefits" of doing the drug, like the fact that it will improve your son's macho social standing or self-image, or make him feel great. Such an explanation may be convincing to your son, or it may appeal to your son's ego, making it harder for him to refuse.

When you talk to your son about refusing drug offers, you can help him imagine the scene realistically by incorporating these facts into the scenario. Rather than picturing a drug dealer in an alley, ask your son to imagine that it's a good friend who is offering the joint, and the friend says, "C'mon, the girls (guys) will think we're cool." Coach your son to explain why doing drugs isn't cool: "It's addictive; it messes with your memory and intelligence; most kids aren't doing it." Another response that might feel comfortable to your son is suggesting an alternative cool activity—"No, thanks, I'm really into staying healthy and looking good, and pot makes you dumb and lazy. Hey, let's go shoot some hoops instead!"

Coaching Girls to Turn Down Drug Offers

When your daughter is offered cigarettes, alcohol, or drugs, it's more likely to be in a private setting, say, at a friend's house, or when alone with an older boyfriend.

Because it happens in an enclosed and intimate setting, it may be harder for your daughter to simply walk away or get out of the situation. When girls are offered substances, the person offering is less likely to give an explanation (e.g., they may simply say, "You want some?"). If there is an explanation, it's usually that the substance isn't that bad for her (e.g., "Don't worry, it isn't going to hurt you"). Unlike your son, when your daughter says no to a drug offer, she may feel more comfortable just saying no. But she should be prepared that saying no may not be enough to get the person offering to leave her alone.

Your daughter is more likely to get drug offers from girls her own age, like a female friend or a young female relative—a sister or a cousin—or from an older boyfriend. These are people that your daughter probably trusts and with whom she feels comfortable and wants to maintain a good relationship.

When you talk to your daughter about how to refuse a drug offer, remind her that she can control her situation. Help her imagine what responses would make her feel confident and comfortable. Use the facts above to paint a few realistic scenarios for her to think about. For example, ask her to pretend her older boyfriend offers her a joint and says, "Would you like to try it? All the girls my age smoke marijuana, it's no big deal." You should acknowledge that saying no may be hard for your daughter because she wants her boyfriend to like her.

Ask her to pretend that she is a girlfriend and that you are your daughter, and have her practice offering you drugs. You may learn something about what your daughter's world is really like. She may

I knew that my daughter would most likely be riding with
a boy to some place where there might be partying/use,
so I gave her options for how to get out of that situation
and get to a safe place. With my son I addressed more
the importance of not driving with substances in the car if
he gave someone a ride that had any, and not riding with
someone under the influence. And I talked to my daughter
more about the skills she might need to get out of a situation
where she was feeling sexually pressured by a boy who
had been using something that would affect his inhibition.
Because my son is older and my children are very close to
each other I had them talk to each other when they had
made mistakes and also to "call each other out" if they
were sensing that one was doing something I would not
approve of. The support system that I taught them when
they were younger carried over into their high school and
college years.

Parent posting on CASA Parent Power discussion forum

say, "Hey, my mom has Vicodin in her bathroom drawer, wanna go
take some?" or "Want one of my brother's Adderall? It will help you
lose weight." You can answer, "No way, that stuff is addictive."

Your daughter may feel more comfortable simply saying no than
debating whether drugs are a big deal. For example, she could practice
saying, "No, thanks," or "I can't do that, my parents would kill me."
Yes, it is okay to encourage your child to use you as an excuse! Sometimes, when your child is uncomfortable with a situation, blaming
Mom and Dad is the easiest way out for both your son and daughter.

THE CONSEQUENCES OF SUBSTANCE
USE DIFFER FOR BOYS AND GIRLS

As I noted in Chapter 1, teens are more likely to follow your rules, and to develop their own responsible decision-making skills, if you involve them in discussions about why you set the rules you do. When it comes to substance abuse, one reason you set clear limits is because you are concerned about your child's health and safety.

You should encourage your daughter to believe that she can keep up with the boys—but not when it comes to smoking, drinking, and using other drugs. Both boys and girls will suffer the consequences of drug use—ill health, addiction, and crippling, or even fatal, disease. But if your daughter goes drink for drink with the boys, she will do more harm to herself than she realizes. Even when using the same amount or less of a particular substance, girls get hooked faster and suffer harsher consequences sooner than boys.

Alcohol is the substance that most teens will use, and it is perhaps the best substance to cite as an example when explaining to your daughter that she is more vulnerable to the effects of substances than her male peers. You and your daughter can discuss the U.S. government dietary guidelines for alcohol. The guidelines underscore the physical difference between the genders—for a woman, nonexcessive drinking is defined as no more than one drink per day; for a man, it is no more than two drinks per day. The impact that one drink has on a woman is equivalent to two drinks for a man. Men's bodies contain more water, which dilutes the alcohol; women have more body fat, which retains the alcohol.

For either gender, drinking more than the limits established by health authorities increases the risk for high blood pressure, stroke, and some types of cancer.

When boys drink alcohol and use other drugs, the consequences tend to be exhibited in more outwardly directed ways. Typical drunken behavior for boys can lead to serious injury and trouble with

Substance-Use-Related Risks
That Are Greater for Girls

Smoking:

- Becoming addicted to nicotine faster and at lower levels of use. In one study, girls became nicotine dependant after three weeks; boys after twenty-three weeks.
- Increased risk of stroke in young women.

Alcohol Use:

- Faster progression from regular alcohol use to alcohol abuse.
- Greater susceptibility to the development of alcohol-related medical disorders, such as liver disease, cardiac problems, and brain impairment.

Drug Use:

- Increased likelihood of becoming addicted to cocaine.
- Increased likelihood of hospitalization from the nonmedical use of pain medications.

Unique Substance-Use-Related Risks for Females:

- Risk of coronary heart disease and stroke for women who smoke and use oral contraceptives.
- Risk of breast cancer for women who drink excessively or begin smoking in early adolescence.

the law. Sons are more likely to drink and drive, and to engage in other physically dangerous conduct, such as climbing things, diving off things, or joyriding on moving vehicles. Sons are also more likely to get into verbal and physical fights with other people while under the influence.

PARENT TIPS

- Get your sons and daughters involved in healthy activities that will satisfy their sensation-seeking impulses.
- Teach your sons and daughters to think critically about whether using drugs to appear cool is in their best interest.
- Monitor your daughter for signs of an eating disorder, anxiety, depression, or poor self-esteem; early intervention is the best prevention.
- Balance peer influence by being fully engaged in your sons' and daughters' lives and by encouraging them to talk to you and to think critically about their friends' smoking, drinking, or drug-taking behavior.
- Prepare your sons and daughters to turn down drug offers by helping them anticipate such offers and practice responding to them.
- Teach your daughter about her higher risk for addiction and substance-use-related illnesses.
- Warn your son about the increased risk of accidents and violence while under the influence of mind-altering drugs.

10

WHAT'S THE RELATIONSHIP BETWEEN ALCOHOL, DRUGS, AND SEXUAL ACTIVITY?

Whatever your moral values or religious convictions, it is important that your children understand how drugs and alcohol are implicated in teen sexual activity.

Whether you set firm rules about abstinence or let your child determine what's best, you should exercise your Parent Power to discuss the relationship between substance use and sex. Substance use can stoke impulsivity, which in turn can trigger risky sexual behavior—the results of which, including pregnancy or contracting a sexually transmitted disease (STD) like HIV/AIDS, could change your teen's life.

Parents hold a range of beliefs when it comes to their teens' sexual conduct. Some think that teen sex is morally wrong—for example, according to the teachings of the Roman Catholic church and evangelical Christians sex outside of marriage is a sin. Other parents believe that their children should not have sex until they are married, or until they are in love, or engaged, or until they are adults. Some parents may believe that teen sex is simply a health issue, not a moral one. Some parents preach abstinence, others are resigned to their teen-agers having intercourse so long as they practice safe sex to protect themselves against pregnancy and disease.

Whatever your personal views, you and your teens need to know that teen drinking and drug use increases the likelihood of risky sexual activity, including having intercourse, having unsafe sex, and becoming the victim of sexual assault. The relationship between teen sex and substance use is so extensive that I believe parents cannot pro-tect their children against the risks of either one without discussing the relationship between the two.

THE COMBUSTIBLE COMBINATION
OF SEX AND DRUGS

Because of their inexperience with both sex and substances, and their still-developing ability to control impulses and appreciate conse-quences, teens are less able than adults to manage the combustible combination of sex and substances. In some cases, they may use drugs or alcohol as a crutch to overcome anxiety, loosen up, make dating more comfortable, or reduce their inhibitions. Some teens drink or get high deliberately, in order to increase the likelihood that they will have sex.

Most twelve- to seventeen-year-olds who use alcohol or illegal drugs, especially those who are frequent or heavy users, have had sex, compared with only a quarter of teens who have never used alcohol or drugs.

CASA, *Dangerous Liaisons: Substance Abuse and Sex,* 1999

The media shares some responsibility here. Movies and television shows often portray people, including teenagers, having instant sex in an emotional vacuum, which makes it hard for children to learn how healthy relationships are developed or what the consequences of having sex will be. Many kids mimic the instant-sexual-gratification scenes they see.

Girls today . . . are coming of age in a more dangerous, sexualized, and media-saturated culture. They face incredible pressures to be beautiful and sophisticated, which in junior high means using chemicals and being sexual.

Mary Pipher, PhD, *Reviving Ophelia: Saving the Selves of Adolescent Girls* (1995)

Self-esteem is another factor. Having low self-esteem puts young people at risk both for experimenting with alcohol and other drugs and for experimenting with sex at an early age. It may lead teens to take drugs or drink alcohol in order to feel better about themselves or to give them the social confidence that they lack. Teens may have sex to gain acceptance, simulate intimacy, or feel desired or loved.

Bolster your children's self-esteem by reinforcing their strengths and providing unconditional love. Teach your child about romantic relationships, about developing trust, communication, and emotional intimacy. This will help your child build healthier relationships. Children who feel valuable and worthy of love are less likely to turn to drugs or sex to seek acceptance.

- Teens under fifteen who have drunk alcohol are twice as likely to have had sex as those who have not.
- Teens under fifteen who have used drugs are almost four times as likely to have had sex as those who have not.

CASA, *Dangerous Liaisons: Substance Abuse and Sex,* 1999

DRUGS, ALCOHOL, AND TWEEN OR EARLY TEEN SEXUAL ACTIVITY

The younger your teen starts to drink or use drugs, the younger your teen is likely to become sexually active. And vice versa—the younger your teen initiates sex, the younger he or she is likely to use alcohol or marijuana.

If you discover that your child is having sex and using substances at an early age, it may signal mental health problems, such as depression. Find a professional that you and your child can talk to confidentially, for example a doctor, social worker, counselor, or clergy member. This trusted confidant may be in a better position than you to unearth the other problems, and to know how to address them.

DRUGS, ALCOHOL, AND DOING MORE THAN PLANNED

Some teens turn to alcohol and drugs to reduce their sexual inhibitions. And it works. But being uninhibited may lead your teen to engage in unintended sexual behaviors that he or she will later regret. Lots of teenagers admit that they have done more sexually than they planned to because they were under the influence of alcohol or other drugs at the time.

Teens often report that their first sexual experience was one they did not plan or foresee, but rather that it "just happened." Alcohol and drugs increase the chance of sex just happening. Having an open dialogue about sex and substances may help your child resist their alluring combination. Use your Parent Power to instill your child with the confidence, self-esteem, and skills needed to avoid occasions and situations that increase the dangers of unintended sexual behavior.

DRUGS, ALCOHOL, AND UNSAFE SEX, PREGNANCY, AND STDS

Teens who use alcohol or other drugs and engage in sexual activity have increased chances of unintended pregnancy and infection with STDs, because teens under the influence are more likely to have unsafe sex.

According to the Kaiser Family Foundation, one in five teens report having unprotected sex after drinking or taking drugs. Teenage girls who smoke pot three or more times a month are less likely to use condoms than those who have never used marijuana.

Most unintended teen pregnancy occurs when one or both of the partners are high on drugs or alcohol. After a decline in the early 1990s, teen pregnancies are once again on the rise.

There is also a relationship between drinking and using drugs and the number of sexual partners a teen has. Teens who drink or use drugs are likelier to have sex with four or more different partners during their teen years than teens who don't drink or use drugs. Having several sexual partners can double a teen's risk of getting an STD.

There is a rise of STD infections among teenagers. One in four teenage girls has an STD. The most common STDs among teenagers are human papilloma virus (HPV), chlamydia, herpes, and trichomoniasis. HPV, by far the most common STD (one in five teenagers has

it), causes genital warts in some cases and can increase a woman's risk of developing cervical cancer.

When talking to your teen about sex and substance use and STDs, make sure to explain that intercourse is not the only sexual activity that might be affected by substance use, nor is it the only one carrying risk. Teens can contract STDs from other forms of sexual contact, such as oral sex and anal intercourse.

DRUGS, ALCOHOL, AND SEXUAL ASSAULT

Substance abuse is a common culprit in sexual assault and rape. Alcohol is found more frequently than any other drug in the systems of those who commit acts of sexual violence: rape, date rape (rape committed by an acquaintance during a voluntary social engagement),

> You don't have a lot of strength [when drunk]. . . . If I hadn't been drunk, it probably wouldn't have happened because I could have gotten up and run out.
>
> Female college student who experienced
> alcohol-related sexual assault

and child molestation. Some perpetrators ply their victims with alcohol and other sedatives in attempts to obtain sex. Perpetrators are more likely to succumb to their impulses to commit crimes when under the influence.

One of the key safety precautions that people can take to reduce the likelihood of becoming a victim of sexual assault is staying sober. Alcohol and other drugs make it harder for potential victims to recognize and escape from dangerous situations, or to resist force. Intoxicated victims are physically vulnerable; sexual assaults are more likely to be attempted and executed when the potential victim is intoxicated because she is less likely or able to fight back, scream for help, or run away from her assailant.

Alcohol is the most common drug used, but your daughter should be warned about other date-rape drugs like GHB and Rohypnol (sometimes called a "roofie"). These drugs can be slipped into the victim's drink, causing dizziness, mental fuzziness, inebriation, and loss of muscle control. They can also erase the victim's short-term memory, making it less likely that the crime will be reported. Teach your teenage daughter to protect herself from date-rape drugs by taking the following precautions:

- Don't drink alcohol.
- Drink soft drinks only from bottles and cans that she has opened herself.

- Pour her own drinks or watch them be poured.
- Never drink from a communal container (such as a punch bowl).
- Always keep an eye on her drink, and get a new drink if she loses sight of the old one.
- Call home if the party's getting out of hand.
- Immediately ask (or even shout) for help if she thinks she has been drugged.

When you talk to your teens about substance abuse and sex, emphasize that one bad choice to drink or get high may lead to sexual activity they will later regret. Practicing abstinence or safe sex is much less likely when their mind is clouded with drugs or alcohol. For daughters, the dangers of unintended pregnancy and of sexual assault can be life-changing. For both sons and daughters, the consequences of STDs are persistent, and in the case of HIV/AIDS, life-threatening.

PARENT TIPS

- Discuss the risky connection between sex and drugs with your children.
- If your teen is sexually active and using substances at a young age (e.g., thirteen or fourteen), seek professional help to identify any underlying problems.
- Teach your teenage daughter to protect herself from sexual assault, including rape and date rape, by not drinking alcohol and by taking precautions against date-rape drugs.

11

HOW CAN I MITIGATE
THE MEDIA'S INFLUENCE?

TRUMP MEDIA MESSAGES
WITH PARENT MESSAGES

Your child's brain is filling up with ideas. That is, in fact, its job. Every day, like a sponge, your child absorbs new information and forms new ideas about the world and how things work. Much of this information comes from the media messages your child is exposed to: Internet sites, billboards, TV shows, text messages, movies, music, magazines, video games. Unfortunately, not all of this information is accurate, and some of it is intended to mislead your child.

In 1964, Marshall McLuhan coined the phrase "the medium is the message" in his book *Understanding Media: The Extensions of Man*, to alert the nation to the power of the electronic image to affect our consciousness. Nowhere is that warning more warranted than with respect to the seduction of the innocent by the barrage of messages glorifying drinking, smoking, and drug use.

In this chapter, I'm going to show you how to use your Parent Power to protect your teens from the excesses of the worlds of advertising, television, music, and entertainment that might otherwise lead them to experiment with various substances.

Starting at a very young age, children are exposed to messages that make smoking, alcohol, and drugs look attractive. They see cartoon characters drinking and smoking, and TV stars popping pills. They listen to songs about smoking pot, and see alcohol and tobacco ads that make people who use these products seem chic and sexy. These messages are so cleverly done, and so common, that your child, and even you, may not notice how persistent they are. But these messages are crafted by sophisticated professionals who know how to reach your kids. The messages can lead your child to think that smoking cigarettes and drinking alcohol are cool.

Unfortunately, children are not always able to sort through the messages they hear, separate the wheat from the chaff and determine which ones are misleading. As a parent, you can teach your child how to distinguish the facts from fiction, the truth from the hype, and how not to be manipulated by tobacco and alcohol merchants.

WHY TEENS ARE IMPRESSIONABLE

Media messages may exert more powerful influences upon adolescents, who are struggling to define who they are and who they hope to be. Adolescents want to be independent, but they also want to fit in with their peers; they develop their own ideas about what it takes to be cool. Unfortunately, your children are going to think that their ideas about being cool are totally original. They probably won't realize just how much advertising and the entertainment media influence what they think about themselves.

We began at an early age to always bring up substance abuse whenever our kids see it in the media. We are careful what we allow them to watch, but we also do not prevent them from seeing the reality of life. We want them to know what is going on in the world around them without glorifying what they see. We want them to understand there are choices they will make and there are consequences to those choices.

Parent posting on CASA Parent Power discussion forum

BALANCING MEDIA INFLUENCES

What can you do to limit the influence of these messages?

- Monitor and limit your child's exposure to the media.
- Look at movie ratings and make sure your children are watching age-appropriate movies (but don't just rely on the rating system).
- Know what your children are doing on the Internet.
- Keep an eye on your child's use of cell phone text messages.
- Watch the TV shows that your kids watch. Even shows geared toward young children may contain misleading messages about smoking, drinking, and drug use.

Children whose parents monitor their media exposure are at lower risk of substance use.

You can control the amount and types of TV and other media that your children are exposed to by setting limits. On average, children and teenagers are exposed to eight and a half hours of media (watching TV, movies, and videos, listening to music, using a computer, playing video games) each day. That's more time spent plugged in to electronic media than most people spend working!

You can provide your children with the right messages to replace the wrong ones. As susceptible as your children's brains are to ideas from the world at large, you are still their most trusted source of information. Consistent messages from you can counteract all of the junk they may hear and see in the media, and the pictures some kids post on their Internet sites.

Talk to your child about media messages. Explain where particular messages come from, who is paying for the commercials on TV, and what they're after. Teach your child that not everything they hear on TV or the radio is sensible, or true, and explain why. Caution them about how smoking, drinking, and drug use are portrayed on social networking (Facebook, MySpace, Twitter) and other Internet sites. You can help your young adolescent make healthy choices by teaching them to think critically about advertising and the media.

Start having these conversations before your children reach the teen years. Children are targeted by the media at a young age, and their heads are filling up with ideas right from the cradle. As soon as they are allowed to turn on a TV and watch it by themselves, be alert to opportunities to tell them about the dangers of drugs and alcohol.

Having discussions about what is being portrayed in the media is key. Our hope is to raise kids that are critical thinkers about these issues. Is it really cool to smoke cigarettes or pot? Is it really sexy to drink/get drunk? Being able to assess a situation or media portrayal accurately within one's own circumstances and drawing one's own conclusions is imperative to being a resourceful and resilient person.

Parent posting on CASA Parent Power discussion forum

THE ADVERTISING ASSAULT
ON CHILDREN

Children are bombarded with glamorous or macho images of substance use. Advertising campaigns of tobacco and alcohol merchants can be extremely effective: At the height of R.J. Reynolds Tobacco Company's Joe Camel campaign, more children recognized the Joe Camel cartoon character than Walt Disney's Mickey Mouse; most kids knew the Budweiser frogs.

Don't be fooled. These companies are spending billions of dollars to get your child to start drinking and smoking at an early age. Why do they target your kids? Because all pushers of addictive or mood-altering products have long known what the public-health community and scientific research has now confirmed—that if they don't get kids to start drinking and smoking when they are young, those kids may never start. Getting kids to experiment—take their first puff, have their first beer (smoke their first joint, pop their first pill, snort their first line)—is key to developing long-term customers and adult addicts.

It's a money-winning formula: Get 'em hooked young and they'll be hooked for life. But wait until they're twenty-one, and you've got one less loyal customer. With more than 400,000 smoking-related deaths a year, the tobacco industry merchants need to get at least 5,000 kids a day to try cigarettes just so they can maintain their markets. For the alcohol industry, there's an even more immediate reason: almost 18 percent of its sales are to underage drinkers.

Remember, parent knowledge is Parent Power. Use advertising examples as teaching moments to help your children resist media messages. Talk to your children openly and honestly about how to decode tobacco and beer media messages. Teach your children that advertising is meant to change the way they think—and teach them how to unscramble these messages and think for themselves.

Let your children know that there are a lot of shrewd salesmen out

> I taught my son from the earliest age that ADVERTISING
> LIES. All advertising is designed to sell something and most
> of it is something no one NEEDS. Its goal is to make you
> think you need it and to increase your desire for it.
>
> Parent posting on CASA Parent Power discussion forum

there who care more about selling their cigarettes, beer, and sweet alcoholic drinks than protecting your child's health. Your adolescents will understand and appreciate that advertising is manipulative, and that with your help, they can resist. The truth® antismoking campaign of the American Legacy Foundation has been successful for this reason. This campaign educates teens about tobacco advertising; it recognizes that teens are rebellious and want to view themselves as independent; it says to kids, "Don't let these guys manipulate you." Like the American Legacy Foundation, you too can use your teens' rebellious nature to keep them smoke and drink free! You can use the American Legacy Foundation website, www.AmericanLegacy.org, and the truth® ads to start a conversation about the media with your kids.

ALCOHOL MARKETING TO TEENS

Alcohol manufacturers spend billions of dollars on television, radio, print, and outdoor advertising, much of it capturing the attention of kids. As the beer, wine, and liquor marketers have long known, exposing children and teens to alcohol advertising influences not only how they perceive drinking, but also whether and how much they intend to drink.

Independent researchers have confirmed that the more children know of beer brands and slogans, the more positively they view drinking—and the more frequently they express a desire to drink beer. In other words, the cumulative impact of advertising is potent—the more ads children see, the more they want to drink. When you watch sports on TV or attend games with your children, notice how many beer ads there are. One in five TV alcohol ads is placed on programming that is geared to twelve- to twenty-year-olds.

Getting your children to drink is so important to the alcohol industry that it devises special products to make alcohol more appetizing. These kid-friendly products include sweet-tasting and colorfully packaged malt or other alcohol-based beverages known as malternatives or alcopops, such as Smirnoff Ice, Mike's Hard Lemonade, and Bacardi Rum Refresher, available in flavors like peach, pineapple, and watermelon. Designed to look like soft drinks, these sweet, fruity alcohol-spiked drinks have become a favorite among teenagers, especially girls. Bacardi has even introduced a diet version of its alcopop, Bacardi Breezers, a play to the female teen obsession to be thin. Girls aged twelve to twenty-one are exposed to twice as many alcopops ads as women over twenty-one. And the alcohol merchants know what they are doing: CASA surveys show that sweetened drinks are the favorite alcoholic beverage among twelve- to seventeen-year-olds.

Products like alcopops are designed not only to be more palatable but also to make drinking easier for your child. They come in bottles with screw-off tops, which are easier to open outside the home, where children are often drinking. They have a higher percentage of alcohol than beer, because companies know that many young drinkers drink to get drunk. And they are sold in small grocery stores and corner markets, places where drinking-age laws tend to be less strictly enforced.

If you suspect that your child has been drinking, smell your child's breath to check for alcohol. But don't limit your investigation to the smell; mints and chewing gum can disguise the odor of alcohol.

MONITOR MOVIES

You may be surprised to learn that movies contain advertising and other messages that influence children and teenagers to smoke, drink, and use drugs. Movies sell images and ideas about lifestyles and personalities; they set the standard for what's cool. Companies know that if their product appears in the right movie scene, sales increase. That's why so many companies, including alcohol and tobacco companies, like to place their products in movies.

Beyond advertising specific products, movies often glamorize smoking, drinking, and using drugs. Teens' smoking behavior is affected by what they see in movies: The more movie characters your child sees smoking, the more likely your child is to start smoking. Close to half of all movies depict a lead character smoking in a way that associates smoking with physical attractiveness and social status. Most R-rated movies show attractive characters smoking. Many of the millions of teens under fifteen who have tried smoking say that they did it because they saw it in a movie.

Chances are your teen is watching more R-rated movies than you think, either in theaters or in your or someone else's home on DVD or cable. R-rated movies contain graphic and mature images of sub-

---

The movie industry has reps that do nothing but sell product placement, from shoes, to computers, to cars, to phones in the movies! We point out the "commercials" for drugs and soda and booze in the movies! "Look at that advertisement!" They now say, "Look at that product placement, Mom!!" The kids hate to see how they are duped into liking something because it was in a movie. When they can spot it, they see what the advertisers are doing.

Parent posting on CASA Parent Power discussion forum

stance use, and studies reveal the relationship between exposure to these images and increased teen smoking, drinking, and other drug use. Teens who see three or more R-rated movies in a typical month are much likelier to smoke cigarettes, drink alcohol, and try marijuana than teens who do not typically watch any R-rated movies.

Even movies geared toward young audiences may contain favorable depictions of smoking and drinking. Here are some scary facts about G and PG-13 movies found in several studies:

- Most films rated PG or PG-13 feature someone smoking.
- In a third of G-rated animated films, alcohol use was associated with wealth or luxury.
- One in five G-rated films associated alcohol with pleasurable sexual activity.

With DVDs, TV clips on cell phones and on YouTube, video-on-demand at the click of a remote, and multiscreen theaters in virtually every neighborhood, it's difficult to monitor your children's viewing habits, but it's worth the effort. Movies that glorify smoking, drinking, and drug use influence impressionable teens and make it more difficult to raise a child who has the will and the skills to say no.

MESSAGES IN MUSIC

Many of Billboard's top hits are anthems to the joys of getting drunk or stoned. One in three popular songs specifically refers to illicit substances. Rap music is by far the worst. Nearly 80 percent of rap songs mention alcohol or marijuana. That's why ministers like Reverend Calvin O. Butts III have criticized rappers and the music industry that records them.

Here are some examples of lyrics of Top 40 songs that children sing along to. In Amy Winehouse's "Back to Black" she sings: "I love you much. It's not enough. You love blow and I love puff and life is like a pipe." Toby Keith in "Get Drunk and Be Somebody" urges ordinary workers to get drunk on payday: "Well all week long I'm a real nobody, but I just punched out and it's paycheck Friday, weekend's here, good God almighty, I'm gonna get drunk and be somebody." And there's 50 Cent's single, "Disco Inferno," in which he sings, "Let's party, everybody bounce with me. Sip champagne and burn a little greenery."

All the iTunes bills come to my e-mail. I check lyrics of songs our son has bought and discuss them with him. He has to pay me back for those that end up being deleted from the hard drive. There's discussion more than mandate.

Parent posting on CASA Parent Power discussion forum

There is a correlation between the amount of time teens spend listening to popular music and their substance-abuse risk. Teens who spend the most time listening to music report repeatedly getting drunk and are at higher risk of using illegal drugs. Learn what music your son or daughter likes and talk to your child about it. Don't let your child spend your money to download or purchase songs that glorify drugs and drinking. Talking to them about the messages they hear in music can make a difference; so will making sure that your children's time is spent engaged in productive activities under adult supervision.

TRIM TELEVISION TIME

Did you know that American children and teens see more ads on television for beer than for fruit juice, gum, skin care products, cookies, sneakers, or jeans?

Not only do we monitor what our children watch on TV and listen to, we also monitor what other families' kids watch and listen to when they're in our presence. We have satellite TV and have blocked and restricted much of what is available and preview almost everything. We also restrict quantity of viewing time.

Parent posting on CASA Parent Power discussion forum

Television abounds with favorable and funny depictions of smoking, drinking, and using drugs. TV characters misbehave all the time without having to face any real-world consequences for their actions. Seeing someone smoking on TV looks cool only because you don't see that person suffering from lung cancer or emphysema later. In the hit television show *Will and Grace*, the character Karen Walker has a closet filled with pills; she is portrayed as a happy-go-lucky woman who happens to be hooked on Vicodin. The show reveals none of the downside of Vicodin addiction, like the fact that without the drug, the addict will suffer withdrawal, including vomiting, diarrhea, painful cramps, and body aches.

It's not just adult characters in adult shows; teenagers are drugging it up in shows that are geared toward teenagers. *Gossip Girl*, the TV show most watched by twelve- to seventeen-year-old girls in 2007 and 2008, chronicles the lives of affluent New York prep school students. The teenage characters routinely smoke, hang out in bars, drink martinis and champagne; they also smoke pot and even snort cocaine. In one episode, two girls abandon a boy who is dying from a cocaine overdose in a hotel room; the deceased boy's parents say the girls weren't to blame because the boy had been using heavily and could have died at any point. The main characters in *Gossip Girl* are not depicted as kids with drinking or drug problems, their antics are portrayed as normal fun for teenagers.

> We also talked about movies and TV shows from the
> beginning of his viewing. We always talked about the
> difference between reality and fantasy. I kept the true
> picture of alcohol and other drug use constantly before him
> so that he could see for himself that this subject is one that
> nearly all movies and TV lie about.
>
> Parent posting on CASA Parent Power discussion forum

Parents, hear this: Every additional hour your teenager spends in front of the TV makes it more likely that he will start drinking, simply because he is exposed to more messages that make drinking look attractive. Research has demonstrated a relationship between the number of hours spent watching TV and music videos (both of which contain more references to drinking than video games) and the likelihood that a teenager will start drinking.

INHIBIT INTERNET ACCESS

While surfing on the Internet, your teenager has access to all sorts of information about drugs, including how to buy and make them. Websites offer detailed descriptions of mind-altering pills, chemicals, herbs, and plants. Chat rooms, such as Bluelight and Erowid, host discussions among drug users about the joys of getting high and how to mix and prepare alcohol and other drugs to get high fast. YouTube, the popular website that allows people to post their own videos, contains numerous images of underage drinkers and pot smokers, as well as instructions on how to do everything from sell drugs and make crystal meth in your kitchen to grow powerful marijuana in your closet. Some videos are spoofs, but they are not labeled as spoofs. Young children watching them receive messages that drugs are fun

Limit the time your teen spends online, put computers in a common area of the house to more easily monitor their use. Set limits on which websites, chat rooms, games, or blogs they can and cannot visit, and discuss consequences for breaking these rules.

White House Office of National Drug Control Policy

and that everyone is doing them. While some adult content on You-Tube is theoretically age restricted, anyone can access it by simply clicking a button that says they're at least eighteen years old, without having to prove it.

As I told you in chapter 4, the Internet is a pharmaceutical candy store. It is full of advertising and offers to sell controlled prescription drugs—pain relievers like OxyContin and Vicodin, depressants like Valium and Xanax, and stimulants like Ritalin and Adderall—without a prescription. The wide availability of controlled, dangerous, and addictive drugs without a prescription on the Internet puts children in danger. More than 90 percent of teens use the Internet, and there are no controls to limit the sale of addictive prescription drugs to them. Today, more teens report abusing these drugs than all other illicit drugs combined except marijuana.

As a parent, you can take steps to make sure your children are not using the Internet to learn about or acquire prescription drugs. Monitor your children's online activities by encouraging computer use in public rooms, such as the living room, rather than in the privacy of your child's bedroom. You can also periodically review the history of the websites that your child has viewed, or install software that will limit or track the content viewed on the computer. Be on the lookout for charges or deliveries from Internet pharmacies—they are not obvious. Look for unfamiliar but generic corporate-sounding names on your credit-card bills and screen your mail for unexpected packages.

Q: Do you limit what your teen sees and does online?
What they post on their MySpace and Facebook profiles?

A: We don't allow our kids to have a MySpace page
(because of privacy concerns), but we have allowed our
son to have a Facebook page, which we monitor on a
regular basis.

A: We have set clear guidelines regarding the use of the
computer. None of the children have Internet access in
their rooms, and the family computer is located in a highly
visible area of our home.

A: Our oldest daughter, who is in high school, maintains
a MySpace page. We monitor it regularly and openly.
We also visit her friends' pages often to stay in touch with
what she is viewing online. We use what we see as a
springboard for conversations about school, drugs, alcohol,
sex, etc.

Parent postings on CASA Parent Power discussion forum

If you allow your child to join a social networking site, such as
Facebook, Twitter, or MySpace, you should do so on the condition
that you'll be able to monitor your child's activities. Many parents
choose to do this by creating their own profile and adding their child
as a friend; this enables the parent to view the content on their child's
profile, such as posted comments, pictures, conversations, relationships updates, and party invitations. My son Joe and I are Facebook
friends of my teenage grandson Joe IV (nicknamed Jack).

> When our oldest daughter began to smoke pot, I found out, in part, because I took her cell phone and read through her text messages. I also got access to her Facebook page and read the comments on the wall. She was hiding pot behind books in the living room bookcase.
>
> Parent posting on CASA Parent Power discussion forum

MOVIE STARS, ROCK STARS, AND ROLE MODELS

Celebrity gossip infatuates America. We are inundated with details about how celebrities eat, dress, date, get high. Look at any magazine rack and you're sure to see headlines about the latest teenage idols and their partying antics. Paris Hilton and Lindsay Lohan became more famous as teenagers for partying than for acting. YouTube videos show Britney Spears apparently high on drugs. Every week another celebrity checks into or out of rehab. Some magazines suggest that rehab is the new in thing for celebrities to do. Far from ruining their careers or reputations, these celebrities become even more notorious as we watch them drink, get high, go to rehab, come out, and go back to their hopped-up lives.

The media stories about celebrity drug abuse offer perfect teaching moments to talk to your children about drugs and drinking. Tell

> Some of the recent headlines involving stars who were once in wholesome family entertainment and have now spiraled out of control have offered the perfect chance to illustrate what can happen when you abuse substances.
>
> Parent posting on CASA Parent Power discussion forum

them: This is not the real world. In the real world, people's lives are ruined when they get addicted to drugs. In the real world, people who drink and drive may wind up dead or in jail for killing someone else in an automobile accident. Use celebrities, like Britney Spears, whose serious problems illustrate how no one—not even the young, rich, and famous—is immune to the dangers of substance abuse. You can also point to the stories of the many celebrities who have died of an accidental overdose—Heath Ledger, River Phoenix, Chris Farley, Anna Nicole Smith, Elvis Presley, Marilyn Monroe, and rappers Pimp C (Chad Butler) and ODB (Russell Jones)—as examples of how dangerous drugs can be.

PARENT TIPS

- Listen to your children's music, watch their TV shows, read the ratings before they see a movie in order to limit your child's exposure to entertainment that has adult content or positive messages about smoking, drinking, or drug use.
- Point out media messages that encourage substance use when you see them. Explain who pays for these messages and what they're trying to make your children believe.
- Monitor your child's use of the Internet.
- Use celebrity drug and alcohol antics as an opportunity to teach your child about the dangers of alcohol and other drug use.

12

HOW CAN I PROTECT
MY KIDS AT SCHOOL?

Walk around the outside of your child's school. Do you see a sign that announces it is a Drug-Free School Zone?

Maybe you and your children pass that sign every day, during school drop-off or pickup. Have you thought about whether the sign is true or false? Does it give you a sense of comfort? Do you think it's baloney?

Have you asked your kids what they think about that sign?

At my organization, CASA, we have.

No, we may not have spoken directly to *your* child, but we have talked to thousands of middle and high schoolers in small towns, medium-size cities, and major urban centers all over the country. And most of them tell us that the words on that sign aren't worth the paint they're printed with.

For more than a decade, CASA has been asking American teens about the presence of drugs within the corridors, classrooms, and on the grounds of their schools. We have surveyed kids in middle and high schools, large and small schools, urban and rural schools, public and private schools, secular and religious schools. What we've learned is shocking: Eight out of ten high school students and four out of ten middle school students say that they've seen schoolmates possessing, using, or dealing drugs, or high or drunk at school.

Even more disturbing, when we have discussion groups of high school juniors and seniors and tell them that 80 percent of high school students say there are drugs in their schools, several of them laugh and say: "The other 20 percent [who say there are no drugs in their schools] must be lying."

For too many American teens, the concept of a drug-free school, that highly touted comforting catchphrase among parents and educators, has become an oxymoron.

WHY PARENTS SHOULD BE CONCERNED ABOUT DRUGS IN SCHOOL

Witnessing Drug Use, Possession, or Dealing Puts Kids at Risk

During the school year, teens spend about half (or more) of their waking hours at school. Whether they spend that time in a drug-free environment or in a drug-infected school—one where drugs are used, kept, or sold—has a big impact on their substance-abuse risk.

Sending your child to a drug-infected school dumps them into

"It's scary," said Mark Scher, principal of East Meadow High School on Long Island, New York. "Kids on the edge will try anything. Now they can get a bag of heroin for less than the cost of going to a movie."

Ann Givens, "Teenage Heroin Use Up," *Newsday*, May 9, 2008

a culture where smoking cigarettes, popping pills, drinking alcohol, and using marijuana, hallucinogens, or other illegal drugs to get high is often accepted as a teen rite of passage. It forces your child to adapt to a climate where peers and older teens make it cool to smoke, drink, get drunk, and use drugs. Kids in schools like these are at much higher risk of falling prey to drug use themselves.

Compared to teens who say there are no drugs at school, those who see drugs at school are:

- Sixteen times likelier to use an illegal drug other than marijuana or prescription drugs.
- Fifteen times likelier to use prescription drugs to get high.
- Six times likelier to get drunk in a typical month.
- Five times likelier to use marijuana.
- Four times likelier to smoke cigarettes.

If you wanted to buy marijuana right now, how long would it take you?

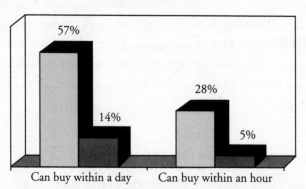

CASA. *National Survey of American Attitudes on Substance Abuse XII: Teens and Parents (2007)*

Remember, availability is the mother of use. This is especially true at drug-infected middle and high schools. Teens at such schools say they can quickly obtain drugs. Compared to twelve- to seventeen-year-olds at drug-free schools, those at drug-infected schools are much likelier to be able to buy marijuana within a day or an hour, about as easily as they can buy candy.

Drugs Infect the Entire Student Body

Next to parents, schools—everything about them, including class-mates—exert the most influence on teen behavior, and that's bad news for most high school students and lots of middle school students.

When schools are infected with drugs, there is a contagion conse-quence that can strike any student, even the school leaders. Substance abuse at schools is not limited to "difficult kids" who exhibit disci-pline problems or fail or cut classes.

CASA research indicates that, all too often, popularity and drug use go hand in hand. The school environment contributes to a culture in which drug use is seen as cool. Teens who say there is drug posses-sion, use, and dealing at their schools are likelier to say the popular kids at their school have the reputation for drinking a lot and using illegal drugs. Kids who say they are among the most popular at their school are twice as likely to say most of their friends drink, smoke, and use pot.

Drugs Threaten Academic Performance

Substance use can adversely affect student performance. Alcohol and drugs physically change the brain and body in ways that can interfere with thinking and make learning and concentration more difficult, thus diminishing academic performance. The more a student uses substances such as alcohol, marijuana, meth, or other drugs, the lower

Some people believe only the bad kids are drinking. It's a
myth that my parents bought into. But it's also the kids who
are heads of the class. No one is immune.

Koren Zailckas, *Smashed: Story of a
Drunken Girlhood* (2005)

his grade point average is likely to be and the more likely he is to drop
out of school. On the flip side, poor academic performance can propel
students toward substance use; if your child is struggling in school,
there is a risk that he may abuse substances to alleviate the pain or
shame of his troubles there.

Alcohol at School

Make sure that your child's school is attentive to drinking as well as
drug use, because the biggest drug problem among teenage students
is alcohol, particularly beer and sweetened alcoholic beverages such as
Smirnoff Ice.

Students who abuse alcohol are less likely to do well in school or
to be committed to doing well in school. Heavy and binge drinkers between the ages of twelve and seventeen are four to five times
more likely to cut classes or skip school. Students at high risk for alcohol abuse are at high risk of being left back, getting suspended from
school, and performing poorly in reading and math.

Marijuana at School

Use of marijuana, the illicit drug of choice among American teens,
is related to lower grade point averages, less satisfaction with school,
negative attitudes toward school, being absent from school, and poor

academic performance. Long-term regular marijuana use can impair memory, attention span, and the ability to comprehend information.

Before the mid-1970s, most people first tried marijuana during college. Today, many first-time users are in middle school.

Early use of marijuana increases the risk of negative academic outcomes. One study found that students who used marijuana before the age of fifteen were three times more likely to drop out of school before age sixteen than students who never used marijuana before age fifteen. Another study found that early use of marijuana (and alcohol and other drugs) predicted early school dropout, failure to graduate from high school, and failure to obtain a college degree.

Most teachers and school administrators attempt to do all they can to keep drugs out of schools, but beware those teachers and administrators who believe that student drug use is no big deal. They are wrong.

CASA's surveys have shown that some middle school teachers think marijuana users can still be good students, and some high school teachers believe that a student who uses marijuana every weekend

---

"I have noticed that Nic is being pulled by the students who the others see as cool," [the teacher] says. "They're the ones who sneak cigarettes and—I'm only guessing— probably smoke pot. They may. But I don't think you have to be overly concerned. It's normal. Most kids try it."

"But," I say, "Nic is only twelve."

"Yes." The teacher sighs. "That's when they try it. There's only so much we can do. It's a force out there. The children have to figure it out sooner or later. Often sooner."

David Sheff, whose son later got into other drugs and almost died of a meth addiction, *Beautiful Boy* (2008)

can still do well in school. But the effects of marijuana on attention, memory, and learning last up to a day or more, so kids who smoke pot on the weekends can experience poor concentration and memory on Mondays and Tuesdays as a result. Most troubling is that so many teachers and principals have a more lax view than do students about the adverse effects of marijuana use on academic performance.

ZERO-TOLERANCE POLICIES

Many schools enforce a zero-tolerance policy regarding alcohol and other drug use. Zero-tolerance policies vary. Some require students who are caught using to be severely punished—suspended or expelled—no matter how small the infraction. Other policies distinguish between use and sale; still others provide treatment and counseling and a second (or third) chance to help the student remain substance free. Zero-tolerance policies are meant to reduce drugs in the school and to make students feel safer on school grounds. They place pressure on parents to keep their kids drug-free, and give children a powerful reason to say no when offered drugs.

But zero-tolerance policies that impose expulsion can discourage students and their parents from speaking up if they suspect that a student is drinking or taking drugs. An unintended consequence of such a policy may be that teens who are experimenting with drugs sink into regular use and students may be less likely to ask for help if one of their friends has a drinking or drug problem or needs medical attention for alcohol- or drug-related reasons.

Find out if your children's school has a zero-tolerance policy. If it does, find out what the consequences of alcohol or other drug use are. And train your child never to leave a friend or classmate who is in trouble or passed out from drug or alcohol use, but to help them or call 911.

Daniel Reardon's son, Danny, was killed in an alcohol-related hazing incident at a school that has a zero-tolerance expulsion policy. Danny's friends could have saved him by calling 911, but they were afraid of getting kicked out of school and so they left him to "sleep it off" instead. Danny never woke up.

HELP YOUR KIDS NAVIGATE THE CHALLENGES OF A DRUG-INFECTED SCHOOL

Put yourself in your child's shoes for a moment and ask yourself: What would it be like to be twelve or fourteen or sixteen years old and witness a drug deal on the football field, or see your friend stash pills in his or her locker? Or be offered pot by an upperclassman? How would you feel? How would you react? Would you say or do anything?

Or try it another way: How would you feel if your coworker on a dangerous construction site were smoking pot or crack, or if someone who works in the office cubicle next to yours or in the stockroom offered you pot? Or suggested that you do a line of cocaine in the bathroom? Would you feel uncomfortable? Suppose that someone was your boss? Would you say or do anything?

If these scenarios make you feel at all uneasy, imagine how difficult it must be for your children to confront such issues at school.

If you have established a comfortable rapport with your kids, you may find it easy to talk to them about drugs in their school. If this is an issue of concern for your kids (as it is for many of the kids we survey at CASA), and if they feel that you are on their side, then they'll likely want to talk to you. Listen closely to your children. Once you raise the issue with your kids, you will have ample opportunity to revisit it. You don't need to accomplish everything in a single talk.

Our research statistics cannot tell you what your child is experiencing or witnessing at school, but they do say something about your children's learning environment. If your daughter or son is in high school, the odds are overwhelming that alcohol and other drugs are there. If your child is in middle school, the odds are at least one in three that he can buy a joint or a pill there. So there's a good chance that your kids are concerned about what's going on in their schools and would like to be able to talk to someone about it.

Be the person they can talk to. Tell them you've read about the problem of drugs in school; ask them if this is what's going on at their school. Find out if this is something they are worried about or have questions about. Let them know you are available to talk to them and that you can help them come up with ways to respond if they see classmates using or if someone offers them drugs. Share with your teenagers the information you learn in this book about the impact of substance use on the developing brain and school performance.

If your child tells you there are no drugs in school, that may be the reality, or it may just be that your child is unaware of the situation. In either case, it's good news. It's also likelier to be the case when your child is young. If your child tells you there are drugs at school, or you suspect that may be the case, encourage other parents to join you in talking to the school principal, headmaster, and teachers. In talking to other parents and to school officials, let them know why you are concerned about drugs at school. Share the information in this chapter with them. You are likely to find them just as concerned, and most schools will take steps to deal with the problem.

For parents who strive to raise healthy, substance-free children, countering the influence on their children of drug-infected school days can be an uphill battle. But do not leave your child to fend for herself in this environment: Acknowledge it if there's a problem in the school and communicate with your child about it.

BEWARE OF SEE-NO-DRUGS, HEAR-NO-DRUGS, SPEAK-NO-DRUGS PRINCIPALS

Some of America's middle and high school principals are living in an unrealistic, sometimes self-serving cocoon when it comes to the presence of drug use in and around their schools. Unlike their students, few principals ever see drugs sold on school grounds. Most claim that their students do not smoke at their schools either. If some students are to be believed, the presence of drugs in schools is as common as pen and paper.

Principals are much less likely than students to admit that drug use is happening on their campuses: Nine out of ten principals say their campuses are drug free, but more than half of students say their campuses are not drug free.

Principals are also less likely to think that drugs are a big problem for students. Principals rank drugs behind family problems and social pressures as the top issues facing teenagers, even though teenagers themselves are more concerned about drugs than anything else.

A former guidance counselor at the school said when she first took the job, she was surprised that the children could purchase drugs in the school hallways or at the park across the street.

Julia Levy, "Tenth-Grade Pupil at Elite School Dies from Overdose of Heroin," *The New York Sun*, September 30, 2004

IT DOESN'T HAVE TO BE THAT WAY: DEMAND DRUG-FREE SCHOOLS

You do not have to accept the presence of drugs as an inevitable part of your child's school experience. And you should not. You have the Parent Power to do something about it.

You do not have to take this struggle on alone. If you are concerned or even just curious about drugs in your child's school, you'll find that many other parents are concerned. Teachers and school administrators also want their schools and students to be drug free.

About half of parents believe that drugs are used, kept, or sold on the grounds of their teen's school. Almost 90 percent of these parents do not hold administrators responsible for this sad state of affairs. Indeed, six out of ten parents believe that making their child's school drug free is not a realistic goal. These parents are wrong!

Parents have successfully pressed for better schools, higher academic standards, and quality education. Some have lobbied to get legislation passed so their children could attend charter schools or receive vouchers to attend parochial schools. If you get a group of parents to understand how having drugs in schools can savage their children's academic achievement and threaten their children's safety and future, they will join you in insisting that your children's schools do everything in their power to ensure that the schools are drug free. The creation of drug-free school environments for our teens is a matter of parental and administrative will.

Parents have the right to demand drug-free schools for their children. Every state requires children to enroll in school (or be home-schooled) until at least age sixteen, seventeen, or eighteen. The state that requires you to send your children to school has an obligation to provide a safe and nourishing school atmosphere for them. You should not let your school, school board, or state or local education authorities force you to send your children for at least half of their

A furious father in Marblehead, Massachusetts, insisted that his son's football coach be suspended for two games because the coach was dipping (chewing) tobacco while coaching, in violation of Massachusetts Interscholastic Athletic Association rules. "The problem is the cancer issue, what it does to kids' teeth. They become addicted to nicotine. It's beyond inappropriate. They think it's cool because he's the coach."

Jessica Fargen, "Spittin' Mad: Irate Dad Wants Tobacco-Chewing Coach Canned," the *Boston Herald*, April 4, 2008

waking hours, nine months out of the year to a place that is infected with drugs.

In talking to other parents, point out that if asbestos were found in your children's school, they would raise hell and refuse to send their children to class until every speck of the dangerous dust had been removed. Moms and Dads who spend thousands of dollars each year to send their children to private schools demand that these schools get their children into Harvard, Yale, Stanford, Holy Cross, Georgetown, and Princeton—and the schools deliver. If they demanded that these schools clear out the drugs, the schools would do that too. If parents made it clear that they care as much about their children's exposure to drugs, alcohol, and cigarettes as they do about their children's exposure to asbestos and College Board test scores, principals and headmasters would clear the fog of tobacco, alcohol, and drugs from their schools.

This will not be an easy task, getting your child's school drug free and keeping it in that condition. Schools have tried a variety of methods: testing all students randomly, testing student athletes, assembling parents and asking their help by not allowing alcohol at parties. But this is a battle worth waging—and it can be won. Use

The Park School in Baltimore, Maryland, instituted a comprehensive program to teach its students to avoid risky and unhealthy behaviors. The Park Connects program brings together parents, teachers, and students for educational programs, such as its Alcohol and Other Drugs seminar, and ongoing community dialogues to promote healthy behaviors among students.

your Parent Power to mobilize other parents and energize the school, teachers, administrators, and students, to make your child's school drug free. You're likely to find that most teachers and administrators will be receptive.

For information about effective substance use prevention and education programs that could be implemented in your community or at your child's school, see SAMHSA's Evidence-Based Programs and Practices database at www.nrepp.samhsa.gov.

WHAT TO DO IF YOUR CHILD'S SCHOOL SUGGESTS MEDICATION

Over the past decade, there has been an increase in the number of school nurses, teachers, and administrators who recommend to parents that their children take medication for emotional and behavioral issues, mainly to treat attention deficit/hyperactivity disorder (ADHD).

For children who suffer from serious ADHD, medication can be a godsend. Kids with ADHD who can't focus or sit still find that the medication makes learning possible. But some overburdened teachers and school administrators may recommend medication in cases where it is not necessary. Because stimulants like Ritalin and Adderall can reduce disruptive behavior, educators—and even parents—may see medication as a quick fix for rambunctious kids and may tend to apply it more liberally than is medically indicated. If a teacher, administrator, or school nurse recommends that your child should be medicated and you have doubts about that recommendation, you can get a second opinion from your child's pediatrician.

If a child is having trouble focusing or is acting out in class, it does not necessarily mean that ADHD is to blame or that medication is the solution. If your child does need medication for ADHD, keep track of your child's pills—his or her classmates may try to get their hands on them. In Wisconsin and Minnesota, more than a third of eleven- to eighteen-year-old students who had been prescribed Ritalin and other ADHD medications reported being approached to sell or trade their drugs. Make sure your child understands that prescription drugs are to be used only as directed by a doctor.

PARENT TIPS

- Talk to your child about whether students are smoking, drinking, or doing or selling drugs at school.
- Bring the information in this book to your school's PTA meeting. Talk to the other parents about joining you in raising the issue with the school leadership.
- Insist that the school take steps to become substance free. Providing a robust substance-abuse-prevention curriculum is important. Establishing and enforcing substance-free rules and policies are also essential. So is providing help for students and their families.
- Aim for a school that helps coordinate support services for students and their families, and insists on parental involvement.

13

HOW CAN I PREPARE MY KIDS FOR COLLEGE?

When you think about preparing your child to go off to college, you may picture yourself buying extra-long, twin-sized sheets, packing up the car with suitcases, lecturing your child about getting the most out of a college education, arriving on campus, and meeting your child's roommate. But you've actually been preparing your child for this moment for years—teaching your child to get a good night's sleep before a big exam, to eat balanced meals, to study hard, to make friends, to spend money wisely. College is about more than picking courses and decorating dorm rooms, it's about making independent decisions.

For many teens, college is a stepping stone toward adulthood, but college campuses are far from mature environments. When you say good-bye and get back in your car, you will leave your new collegian surrounded by thousands of other teenagers, all free from any parental supervision, almost all for the first time in their lives. Due in part to this newfound freedom, your child will face a new world of challenges and temptations.

As parents, preparing your children for college means vesting them with the values and skills to face those challenges, to make smart decisions, and to avoid dangerous temptations and threats. Among those temptations and threats will be alcohol and other drugs.

Sending your children to college without coaching them about how to deal with drugs and alcohol would be like giving them the keys to the car without teaching them how to drive. If they get behind the wheel, they could cripple or even kill themselves. When faced with unlimited access to drugs and alcohol—and plenty of free time to party—unprepared college students can ruin their lives or accidentally end them.

That first year of college is the most dangerous transition time your child is likely to confront. This is why your influence is more important now than ever: 70 percent of college students say that their

"I went on spring break a boy and came back an alcoholic."

parents' concerns or expectations influence whether or how much they drink, smoke, or use other drugs. So even though you won't be on campus with your children, you will have a big impact on their conduct.

In this chapter, I'll explain the steps you should take to prepare your children for college. First, I'll describe the college substance-use scene and its dangers, so that you and your children will know what to look out for. Second, I'll give you tips about how and when to talk to your children about substance use on college campuses. Then I'll give you some suggestions for ways to help your children pick a college and choose their college housing. Last, I'll tell you how you can stay engaged and continue to empower your children to make good choices once freshman year begins.

EDUCATE YOURSELF AND YOUR TEEN ABOUT SUBSTANCE ABUSE ON COLLEGE CAMPUSES

If you needed to sit down as you read about the situation in our high schools, you'd better get back into that seat as you learn about the world your child will enter in college.

Perhaps you are inclined to think that kids will be kids, and that college is the time when they should be permitted to take a walk on the wild side. Maybe you're thinking back to your own college years, the drinking and partying that took place: "Sure, we got a little crazy,

---

Looking at national trends, we know that alcohol abuse is the single greatest health issue affecting college students.

Margaret Garner, director of health and wellness, University of Alabama, quoted in *The Crimson White*, March 26, 2007

Getting alcohol is like getting water at my school.

College student in CASA focus group

but so what? We had fun, we graduated, and now we're all healthy, productive adults. The same will be true for my kids."

What you may not be thinking—but what you should know— is that the college experience today is vastly different from the days when you were a student. In your day, male college students may have been more prone to excessive drinking than females; today, women have caught up and are drinking just as recklessly. Four out of every ten college students binge drink. Many college campuses are encircled by bars that sell beer and alcohol at low prices to attract students. Fake IDs are a dime a dozen.

The mix of drugs that is available on college campuses today is new and ever-changing, and the dangers of these drugs are misunderstood and underappreciated by students. Many colleges have abandoned any parental role toward students; others have reduced their in loco parentis (standing in the place of parents) roles. Technology gives students greater access to instant information—about parties and drugs and how to get them and use them. And students have more time than ever to party; they can set their schedules so that they have no Friday (or even Thursday) classes and fewer morning classes. The weekend can begin on Wednesday or Thursday evening, and extend far into Monday. The amount of free time your child can have in college will be a dramatic lifestyle change that can set the stage for abuse of alcohol and other drugs.

To prepare your child for college, you need to know what he's getting into. I'm going to paint a detailed picture for you.

New Mix of Pot, Pills, and Powders

There's a new mix of pot, pills, and powders on college campuses today. Nine in ten college students say alcohol (for those who are underage) is easy to obtain and two-thirds say addictive prescription drugs (without a doctor's order) and marijuana are easy to obtain.

The abuse of prescription drugs among college students has exploded. On some campuses, prescription drug abuse is more common than marijuana use. College students know well the abuse ("party") potential of prescription drugs like Ritalin, Adderall, Vicodin, Oxy-Contin, Xanax, and Valium. Adderall and Ritalin are abused by college students to help them study or write papers. Vicodin and OxyContin are abused on college campuses by kids looking to get high. Xanax and Valium are abused to relax, chill out, and sometimes to sleep. Often these prescription drugs are mixed with alcohol.

The Internet is where college students often turn to get information about any number of things, including prescription drugs. There are chat rooms focused on discussing side effects, dosage amounts, where to obtain, and how to abuse prescription drugs. College students with their own post office boxes can order, without a prescription, highly addictive controlled substances like OxyContin and Vicodin from the Internet. A staggering 89 percent of sites selling controlled prescription drugs have no legitimate prescription requirements.

There's a consistent rise in prescription-drug and alcohol abuse on college campuses. [It's] nearly out of control, kind of a constant, partying subculture. . . . It's a phenomenon of college. It's a phenomenon of our society.

Luke Nasta, director of Camelot Counseling Centers, in the *Staten Island Advance*, March 16, 2007

Women Drinking More Than Ever

Women on college campuses today are drinking lots more than their mothers ever did. When asked why, women say they drink to reduce stress and keep up with the boys. They also say that the pressure to have sex leads them to use alcohol as a disinhibitor to help deal with that pressure. A generation ago, college women were more inclined to forgo alcohol for fear of letting down their guard and ending up having sex. Today's college women (and men) are likelier to use alcohol to shed their inhibitions and increase the likelihood of "hooking up" (a student euphemism for sexual activity without any commitment).

One of the points you should make with your daughter is that getting drunk (or high on drugs) puts her at higher risk for sexual assault. Alcohol is far and away the campus's number one date-rape drug. Roughly one in twenty college women are raped each year; most of them are drunk at the time of the assault.

Maria attributes the hook-up culture first and foremost to a lot of drinking. This enables students to do things they won't remember the next day. "I know some girls have hopes that it will turn into more if they hook up with a guy," Maria says, expressing a common opinion about why women are willing to hook up that I heard repeated many times by both the men and women I interviewed. But "some girls just do it because they are drunk and they think it is fun, and boys just go along with whatever girls want to do, and [the boys] obviously want to say they hooked up with a girl that night. Guys are into that."

Donna Freitas, *Sex and the Soul: Juggling Sexuality, Spirituality, Romance, and Religion on America's College Campuses* (2008)

Universities Are Not Surrogate Parents

At some universities, especially large institutions, students have little opportunity to form personal relationships with their professors, counselors, or other adults on campus. In such environments, mostly for the first time in their lives, your children are left to their own devices, without the benefit of adult supervision to encourage responsibility. No one is hovering over them like parents to make sure they don't abuse drugs and alcohol. However, some institutions of higher learning, such as Notre Dame, continue to foster a culture of stewardship with respect to their students' behavior and development.

The supervisory relationship between many institutions of higher learning and their students (who are overwhelmingly under twenty-one) is shaped, in large part, by the school's degree of legal liability for the consequences of student behavior. Increasingly, courts are holding universities liable for foreseeable harms to students, including alcohol-abuse related injuries, sexual assaults, and deaths, if the university failed to use reasonable care to prevent the harm. However, the university's duty of care does not extend to off-campus incidents, including fraternity- or sorority-related drinking events. As a result, some universities seek to avoid liability by banning parties on campus and forcing students to move them off campus, or by imposing regulations and policies aimed at curbing alcohol and drug use by students.

Few schools keep careful track of alcohol- and substance-related incidents among students, and they rarely notify parents of such incidents. If the substance-related incident involves disciplinary action, only about a third of schools notify parents.

Federal education law requires colleges and universities to keep track of the school's enforcement of consequences for violations of the school's drug and alcohol policies. But the standards of what conduct is reportable vary, and there is considerable underreporting and little, if any, auditing of these reports by the U.S. Department of Education.

Many parents do not want to know if their children in college experience legal difficulties resulting from underage alcohol or drug use. When the University of Missouri attempted to institute a parental-notification policy as part of a broader effort to reduce student substance abuse, parents fought back. Many said that they send their children to college to experience, as they did, "life as it really is," and that drinking is part of the college experience and the real world. Other parents worried that being notified of their children's substance-related legal troubles might harm their relationship with their children. In the face of this denial and resistance from parents, we instituted a less strict parental-notification policy than we otherwise would have.

Manuel T. Pacheco, PhD, former president, University of Missouri System and University of Arizona

Colleges and universities are also required to publish certain information related to drug and alcohol crimes committed on and around campus, but only if such crimes lead to an arrest or a documented disciplinary action by the university. At most schools the true picture of student substance abuse remains hidden, but it is nonetheless very real.

Instant Communication = Instant Access

Cell phones, BlackBerries, iPhones, laptops . . . college students are connected in more ways than ever before. Being connected means always knowing where the party is and where the drinking games and open beer kegs, jello shots, vodka, marijuana, and other drugs are. With campuses fully wired for the Internet, students can order drugs online from their laptop in class and have them sent to their mail box or delivered to their dorm room. There is no longer the need to go off campus or even down the hall in search of drugs. Using a cell phone, or even MySpace or Facebook, students can text message their drug dealer or friends to order whatever substances they want and have them delivered straight to their rooms. In California, one drug dealing student was busted after sending a mass text message to his "faithful clients" promoting a cocaine sale.

Students Have More Time to Party

The urge to let loose and party on the weekend is natural, because Saturdays and Sundays are days when you don't have to get up and go to work. But for many college students, every day is the weekend. Some students choose classes that meet only in the afternoon so they can go out drinking every night. Some universities have stopped holding classes on Friday altogether, because so many students are partying Thursday night and skipping classes on Friday, and because so many faculty want long weekends or another day for consulting or research. The result is that the weekend extends at least from Thursday to Monday afternoon. Not having to get up and go to class on most days encourages students to spend more evenings drinking and doing drugs.

A DETAILED PICTURE OF COLLEGE SUBSTANCE USE

Substance abuse is rampant and epidemic on our college campuses. We're not just talking about kids partying a little too hard or occasionally having a little too much to drink. We're talking about a significant segment of our nation's best and brightest having a diagnosable substance-abuse problem.

Less than 10 percent of the general population (twelve and older) meets the medical diagnostic criteria for alcohol and/or drug abuse or dependence. In contrast, more than double that number (23 percent) of full-time college students meets the same clinical criteria. Each month, almost four million full-time college students—50 percent— binge drink, abuse prescription drugs, and/or abuse illegal drugs.

College drinking and drug use are, simply stated, out of control:

- Ask the mothers of the 1,700 college students who die each year from alcohol-related causes.
- Ask the fathers of the almost 100,000 female college students who become the victims of sexual assault or rape each year due to alcohol abuse.
- Ask the nearly 700,000 college students who are assaulted each year as a result of alcohol abuse.

Am I trying to scare you? No.

But I do want to splash some cold water on your face so you wake up to the fact that college drinking and drug use is a serious matter. The point is not for you to be frightened, but for you to be informed. Remember, parent knowledge is Parent Power.

Parents Patty and Rick Spady had no idea about the culture of college drinking when they sent their daughter Sam off to Colorado State University. In high school, Sam was captain of the cheerleading squad, class president, an honor student, and homecoming queen. In her sophomore year, nineteen years old, Sam was found dead over Labor Day weekend after a night of binge drinking. Investigators believe Sam consumed as many as forty vanilla-flavored vodka drinks that night.

ABC News, June 12, 2006

I've actually met more kids here at NYU that have been sent to the hospital or emergency rooms because of alcohol poisoning than I've ever experienced back at home. I think it's kind of ridiculous how kids lose control of themselves.

Jordan Sun, NYU student, on NY1 News, March 15, 2007

You might be thinking, however, aren't college students practically adults? A lot of adults drink or take pills to relieve tension; they don't have a problem, so what makes college students so different? It is true that most adults who drink are not problem drinkers and most adults who take pills will never become addicts. But college students are different from the average adult. The average adult over twenty-five has a fully developed brain, and usually a full-time job and family responsibilities. College students are young—some are only seventeen when they start. Their brains aren't fully developed and they are more susceptible to addiction than an adult. College students also have the time and opportunity to party, constantly if they want.

A Warning About Drinking Games

Ever hear of Beer Pong, Beirut, Flip Cup, Keg Race, Power Hour, or Edward Fortyhands? If those names don't make sense to you, they definitely will to your college-age son or daughter. They're the names of popular drinking games on college campuses.

In Beer Pong (also called Beirut), players throw a ball across a table, trying to get it into a cup—if the player gets it in, the opposing team has to drink all of the beer in that cup. Flip Cup is an alcohol relay race in which each team member must chug the entire contents of the cup before him, then set the cup down on the edge of the table and try to flip it so that the cup lands on its opposite end. Once the

A College Hazing Tragedy

In August, 2004, Lynn Gordon Bailey, Jr., known to family and friends as Gordie, arrived for his freshman year at the University of Colorado at Boulder, Leeds School of Business. One month later, he was found dead, lying facedown on the floor of the Chi Psi fraternity house.

Gordie was only eighteen years old when he died. He was a popular, successful student and athlete. In his first few weeks at the university, Gordie had been named to the club lacrosse team. In high school, at Deerfield Academy in Massachusetts, Gordie was cocaptain of the varsity football team and a star on the school's New England championship lacrosse team. Gordie also excelled in music and drama; at his high school graduation he received the Class of 2004 Award of Excellence in Drama.

The night before his death, Gordie and twenty-six other pledges, dressed in coats and ties for bid night, were taken blindfolded to the Arapaho-Roosevelt National Forest. When the blindfolds were taken off, the pledges were seated around a bonfire. They were given four 1.75 liter bottles of whiskey and six 1.5 liter bottles of wine and told they had thirty minutes to drink them. After consuming all the alcohol, they returned to the fraternity house. Gordie, visibly intoxicated, was placed on the couch to sleep it off. After Gordie passed out on the couch, the brothers proceeded to write on his body, another fraternity ritual. The next morning, Gordie did not wake up.

The Gordie Foundation created The Circle of Trust, a campus program to educate students about the dangers of binge drinking and encourage them to get help for friends in trouble. www.gordie.org

cup is successfully flipped, the next teammate must drink and flip, and so on, until the entire team has done it. Edward Fortyhands is a drinking game in which each player duct-tapes a forty-ounce bottle of alcohol (usually malt liquor) to each of his or her hands and is not allowed to remove them until both bottles have been consumed.

A common college twenty-first birthday game is to encourage the birthday girl (or boy) to consume twenty-one drinks in the first hour or so after midnight.

The goal of these games is straightforward: Get drunk and get drunk fast. This is achieved by forcing the participants to chug alcohol (drink a large amount in a short period of time). Chugging alcohol bypasses the body's normal defense mechanisms (feeling full, sick or tired, and vomiting). That's why the amount of alcohol consumed during these games can so easily reach dangerous levels, causing alcohol poisoning and sometimes death.

The devastating effect of these drinking practices on campus has forced several schools and communities to start banning drinking games. Unfortunately, many schools permit them or look the other way, and many bars around campuses encourage them.

Talk to your kids about the dangers of drinking games before they

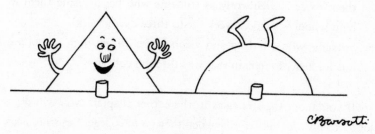

"I win. I win."

The circle passes out after losing a drinking game to the triangle.

leave for college. One night of Edward Fortyhands may seem like a fun way to spend a few hours, but it can quickly spiral out of control and land your teen in the hospital—or the morgue.

START PREPARING YOUR CHILDREN IN HIGH SCHOOL

Your Parent Power to influence your kids positively will persist through the college years—especially if that influence is cultivated before college starts. Parents of students about to enter college have the best chance to prevent substance abuse by their children if in middle school and in high school they developed a positive, open, nurturing relationship, demonstrated explicit disapproval of substance use, and had a history of monitoring their children's behaviors and not being overly permissive.

The truth is that most college students who drink and use drugs in college were doing so in high school—or even before.

- Two-thirds of college students who drink alcohol or use illicit drugs began using them in high school. Almost one in ten began using in middle school.
- College students who began using drugs in middle school use them twice as frequently as students who began using them in high school (six days a week versus three days a week).
- Students who are drug and alcohol free during high school are much likelier to remain that way through college.

If you adopt the strategies in the earlier chapters, you will do a lot to keep your children safe when they go to college. Resisting peer pressure and avoiding risky situations are acquired skills and the best time to teach them is when your teen is living at home with you. If you can keep your son or daughter drug and alcohol free before going

We are aware as an institution, and have been aware, of the changing dynamic over the past fifteen years. We understood that we're getting students who have been drinking in high school, but to hear that numbers are so high is alarming.

Zenobia Hikes, Virginia Tech's vice president for student affairs, in the *Roanoke Times & World News*, March 16, 2007

to college, that child will have the best chance of staying sober over the next four years.

Even if you have not consistently discussed the dangers of substance use in the past with your children, brief parent-teen interventions about your expectations and the dangers of substance use and abuse prior to your child entering college can help to form a baseline for appropriate and healthy behavior in college. Both parents need to be involved and to present a united front when it comes to expectations about substance abuse.

HELPING YOUR TEEN PICK A COLLEGE AND COLLEGE HOUSING

Choosing a college is among the most important decisions you and your child will have to make. You have the Parent Power to be quite influential in the choices that your children make in the process of selecting, preparing for, and attending college. Parents are consulted more often than peers, other adults, teachers, college resources, or media for every possible college-related choice: academic, institutional, personal, social, and financial.

FINDING THE RIGHT CAMPUS
ENVIRONMENT

Colleges and their surrounding communities often create or enhance an environment that enables or even promotes substance abuse among students. Attending a college where the culture encourages substance abuse can threaten the health and future of your child.

Alcohol, tobacco, and other drugs—both prescription and illicit—are relatively easy to obtain on campuses. Student residences often are awash in alcohol; bars and other alcohol and tobacco retailers frequently surround the campus. Many campuses and communities lack strong and well-enforced policies on substance use.

Different schools have different inherent risks for substance abuse; "party schools" often live up to their reputations for heavy alcohol and drug use. When your child starts the process of picking a college, you can take a look at the lists of top party schools on websites like www.princetonreview.com/bestcolleges/parties.aspx.

Party schools are usually emblematic of widespread binge drinking and drug use, an uninhibited fraternity, sorority, or other club life, and less focus on getting a good education. If your son or daughter is only interested in attending a big party school, ask why. If your child is thinking only about the potential for an exciting social life,

---

When the topic [at the orientation for parents of freshmen] turns to how parents might talk with their child about drinking, one parent in the back will say, "Oh, but kids will be kids," and everyone will laugh.

Wren Singer, director of freshman orientation, University of Wisconsin, in CASA Report, *Wasting the Best and the Brightest: Substance Abuse at America's Colleges and Universities*, 2007

There's a lot of reasons that, you know, the students are finding reasons to drink—when they're done with an exam, or there's lots of bar specials all the time, too, cheap, cheap beer. Cheap shots. Anything.

Amy Gnotek, a senior at Michigan State University, on CNN's *Lou Dobbs Tonight*, March 15, 2007

remind him of some of the negative consequences of substance abuse on campus like vandalized rooms, rapes and sexual assaults, vomit in the dorms, lack of sleep, or having to rush a drunk roommate to the hospital. You can refuse to pay for your child to attend such a school.

Confirm whether the schools your child is considering have peer education or university-sponsored student support programs to deal with substance abuse, and educate students about the dangers of binge drinking, hazing, and alcohol poisoning.

During the school-selection process, you should research the alcohol and drug policies of colleges that your child is considering. Find out what policies the school has for protecting students from substance abuse. You can look many of them up online at: www.collegedrinkingprevention.gov/policies. When you go on a campus tour, ask questions about the social scene: Does the school have alcohol-free events on campus? Are fraternity and sorority parties the only (biggest) social things to do? Does getting accepted into a fraternity or sorority involve dangerous hazing or drinking activities? Are there substance-free dorms? Is smoking allowed in public places?

Find out if classes are held on Fridays and if students can arrange their class schedules to avoid Friday and morning classes. Find out if the administration keeps track of how many students have been hurt or injured from substance abuse in addition to keeping legally required records of violations of school policies or laws. What actions, if any, does the school take when students are caught with drugs or

Some universities have taken steps to curb binge drinking. Find out whether the schools your child is considering have taken steps or adopted programs or policies to reduce substance use and drinking on campus, such as:

- Banning smoking on campus.
- Providing mandatory education about alcohol abuse and addiction to incoming freshmen.
- Supporting peer education programs.
- Offering substance-free housing options.
- Providing counseling for students who are substance abusers or become addicted to alcohol or drugs.
- Banning alcohol in dorms, in most common areas, at on-campus student parties and at college sporting events.
- Offering alcohol-free events and activities.
- Requiring trained servers where alcohol is offered and banning open kegs.
- Closing down fraternities or sororities where drinking is excessive.
- Reporting all substance-use infractions of students to parents.

alcohol? You should also find out what steps the school is taking to restrict dangerous drinking games on campus and in the surrounding community.

How Readily Available Is Alcohol?

Here's another rule of thumb I have for you: The greater the number of alcohol outlets available to students, the greater the likelihood of problem drinking.

Having a bar on campus increases the risk that underage students will drink and binge drink. Students in wet environments, in which binge drinking is common and alcohol is readily available and cheap, are more likely to become binge drinkers than students in dry environments, where alcohol is hard to obtain and/or drinking is discouraged. In wet environments students can obtain alcohol for free at parties or at deeply discounted prices from bars catering to college-age clientele. College bars offer specials designed to draw heavy-drinking crowds. Some bars have ladies hours, during which girls can drink cheaply or for free in the early evening. The hope is that men will be attracted to the bar later, when it is full of tipsy women, a situation fraught with danger of sexual assaults and date rape. Other bars offer drink specials so cheap that anyone can afford to get wasted. And getting wasted is the goal; these bars prosper on binge drinking.

When visiting college campuses with your children, you should take note of the number of bars and liquor stores in close proximity, and you should remind your son or daughter of your expectations

---

This month, searchers combing the Mississippi river [in La Crosse, Wisconsin] found the body of the eighth college-age man in nine years to disappear from one of the taverns and turn up dead in the river. La Crosse officials have debated for years how to keep drunken students safe . . . [in a] town with three colleges, three rivers, and three-dollar pitchers of beer. . . . The Vibe, where . . . [the man] was last seen alive, offers an all-you-can-drink special for five dollars. Shots are a dollar. A sign in the bar's window proclaims: "You're not drunk if you can lie on the floor without holding on."

"Hard-Drinking College Town Struggles to Curb Drowning," *The New York Times*, October 23, 2006

The University of Maryland's college newspaper has carried ads from a bar that offers pints of beer for a penny to college women from nine to eleven on Saturday evening as a way to attract them—and men who aren't admitted until after eleven, when the women are well-lubricated with alcohol.

---

regarding underage drinking. Alcohol use is common on many campuses, but it does not mean that excess drinking and binge drinking has to be the norm.

Is the Health Clinic Keeping Kids Healthy?

For many students, visiting the student health center may be their first trip to the doctor without parental supervision.

College students can easily obtain prescription drugs on campus by faking symptoms and getting a prescription from the school health clinic. They can find out how to fake symptoms on the Internet. Many students say that they can get a prescription for Adderall just by saying they need help concentrating.

Students in CASA's focus groups report the ease of obtaining prescription drugs from school health centers and how a student with a legitimate prescription for a painkiller or a stimulant medication may use some of the dose but then share the rest with friends. Several students mention receiving large amounts of opioid pills for athletic injuries or dental problems, using only a few to ease their legitimate pain, then sharing the excess medication with classmates or selling it to them.

Talk to the administration or the staff at the health center to learn the clinic's policies for prescribing medications and monitoring their use, and its practices for dealing with substance-abusing students.

CONSIDER HEALTHY HOUSING OPTIONS

Substance-Free and Single-Sex Dorms

In looking at colleges with your child, find out whether there are any substance-free dorms where smoking, drinking, and drugs are banned.

More and more, students choose to live in such substance-free housing. What substance-free housing does best is protect students from experiencing some of the adverse consequences of other students' substance abuse, particularly their binge drinking. Nobody wants to clean up after a drunk roommate or have drug users crashing in their bed. Substance-free housing can be a great way to avoid these problems and stay safe while still enjoying college. Although students living in substance-free dormitories do sometimes drink, they generally drink less, and less often.

Among students living on campus, those who live in coed dorms report more alcohol-related nuisances and binge drinking than those in single-sex dorms. When the time comes to pick housing for freshman year it is a good idea to encourage your son or daughter to consider substance-free housing or single-sex dorms. Neither choice will preclude going to parties and enjoying college life, but either choice can reduce some of the nastier consequences of substance abuse in dorm life.

Don't Tolerate a Substance-Abusing Roommate

Having a roommate who abuses drugs or alcohol can have a negative impact on your son or daughter. Adjusting to new roommates is an integral part of the college experience, and the housing office can often be hesitant about haphazardly changing roommates. But if a roommate's drug or alcohol abuse is putting your child at risk, it is your responsibility as a parent to speak with the administration to resolve the situation promptly to protect your child.

Consider Living at Home

Students whose parents live close to their university may choose to live at home and commute to school. Research shows that students who live at home during college are less likely to drink or use other drugs than students living on campus. Although moving away from home is an important step in a student's personal development, for some high-risk students, living at home, at least during freshman year, can be an effective way to prevent substance abuse.

Get to Know Your Child's Residential Advisor

If your child spends freshman year living in a dorm, chances are there will be a residential advisor (RA), a faculty member or an upperclassman who lives in the dorm and serves as a big brother or big sister to the freshmen. A conscientious RA can be a resource to talk to while your child is busy on move-in day, and can give you an assessment of the extent of alcohol and drug use on campus. Establishing a relationship with your child's RA, even if it's just sharing e-mail addresses, can be helpful for you and your child during freshman year. The RA is likely to know who your child's friends are, how much drinking and partying they do, and if they have started using drugs and alcohol. Whether it is the RA or someone else, maintaining a relationship with an adult on campus who is in contact with your child can be an important part of helping your child avoid harmful behavior.

PARENTAL ENGAGEMENT
CONTINUES INTO COLLEGE

The nest may be empty, but your job's far from over. Your Parent Power doesn't end when college begins.

Staying engaged and continuing to incorporate the lessons

from this book will help keep your sons and daughters safe as they start this significant chapter in their lives. Let the college officials know that you expect them to discourage drinking and drug use and that you want to be notified if your child is found to be abusing any substance.

Here are some additional things you should consider once college begins.

Spending Money

If you're paying your child's credit-card bills or sending your child spending money, keep an eye on how much your child is spending. A sudden increase in spending habits could indicate substance abuse. Also, look over the credit-card bills carefully—illegal prescription drugs and other drug paraphernalia may show up as cosmetics, food, soap, or other innocuous and random items. Keeping track of how the money you send is being spent can be helpful in spotting signs of potential substance abuse.

If you send your child spending money, make sure the amount is moderate. As in high school, teens with too much disposable income are more likely to be substance users.

Find New Ways to Stay in Touch

Maintaining a relationship with your child during college is an important step in keeping your child substance free. Although college should be a time for your children to grow on their own, there are still many opportunities for parent participation that won't feel overbearing or intrusive. Try going to parents' weekend or a football game on campus. Even dinner at a nice restaurant will be a welcome opportunity for your son or daughter after a few months of cafeteria food.

While you are at home you can still keep in touch, but keep in mind that you may have to be more flexible. Students may not always

I had occasion to visit the emergency room a few times at the University of Arizona. I was surprised that students who were being treated for bruises from fights that happened while they were drunk implored me not to tell their parents they were intoxicated. It gave me a strong sense that the possibility of parental displeasure about their children's behavior and drunkenness can have a moderating effect on students' behavior in many cases. Parents can positively influence their children's behavior at college if they tell their children what their expectations about substance use are and that they have asked to be informed by the school if the children's behavior in this regard is unacceptable.

Manuel T. Pacheco, PhD, former president, University of Arizona and University of Missouri System

be able to chat on the phone or in person so it helps for parents to learn how to communicate through e-mail or text message. Sending a quick e-mail or text message takes only a couple of seconds, but it will let your child know you are there while still giving them the necessary space to grow.

Many students say they are aware of the adverse consequences of substance use, including lower academic performance and sexual violence; but this knowledge does not seem to be enough to dissuade them from abusing alcohol, smoking, or using other drugs. Consistent messages from parents—of caring and of expectations—will have greater impact than any public service message.

PARENT TIPS

Before College

- Discuss your expectations and the dangers of substance abuse with your children

When Picking a College, Consider the Following

- Is the campus smoke free?
- Does the college have a clearly defined alcohol policy that is consistently enforced?
- Does the college ban alcohol and other drugs in public areas?
- Does the college sponsor dry social activities?
- Does the college allow alcohol to be involved in rushing for fraternities and sororities?
- Is attending fraternity and sorority parties the dominant social activity?
- Is the college surrounded by a high density of bars and liquor stores?
- Are there substance-free or single-sex housing options?
- Does the college keep track of alcohol and other drug incidents?

When Your Child Goes Off to College

- Let the school know you want to be informed if your child is involved in an alcohol- or other drug-related incident.
- Keep an eye on your child's spending habits.
- Communicate regularly with your child—and continue to discuss the temptations and dangers of drinking and drugs.

PART III

CONFRONT IT

14

THE SIGNS OF USE—WHAT
TO DO IF YOU SEE THEM

Plants can't tell you when something is wrong, but if you are a gardener you can detect signs of ill health in your plants by observing them. You can inspect a plant's leaves for signs of trouble or disease, and the leaf will sit still in your hand as you check its texture, color, and health. If there are signs of a problem, you can buy a spray treatment at the store to fix it, and the plant will not resist your spraying.

But children are not plants. Though children can talk, they won't always tell you when something is wrong. If your child starts drinking or experimenting with drugs, it won't necessarily be obvious. You won't see black spots or fungus growing. Your son or daughter is more likely to hide it than to tell you. If your child develops a substance-abuse problem, there are no quick fixes, no sprays, to cure it. Indeed, your child may resist your efforts to deal with the problem.

The early signs of substance use are subtle, if not obscure. That's why it is so important for you to recognize the risk factors that often precede use. If you respond to the risk factors early on, you will reduce the likelihood that your child will ever start using drugs. These risk factors include having a genetic predisposition, a learning disability, an eating disorder, or an emotional, developmental, or behavioral problem, being stressed out, feeling perpetually bored, having a family member who uses, lacking self-esteem, exhibiting sensation-seeking behavior, having sex at an early age, and dating someone several years older. Timely and consistent parental engagement can mitigate these risk factors; lack of it will increase your child's likelihood of drinking and using drugs.

SPOTTING THE SIGNS OF USE

Early signs of substance abuse are often indistinguishable from normal teenage behavioral changes, such as mood swings, erratic sleeping patterns, an increased demand for privacy, or changes in hobbies, interests, or friends. So how can you differentiate between normal teenage behavior and indications that your child might be using drugs and needs your help? It's a matter of degree. You should be concerned about changes that are sudden or drastic; these may indicate that something is wrong, drug-related or otherwise. You should also be concerned if several changes occur simultaneously.

You are more likely to detect the early signs of use if you are engaged in your child's life, know your child's world, and have established a foundation of communication that will allow you to discuss any issues that arise. A parent's best early detection device is an ongoing dialogue with teens concerning their thoughts, feelings, friends, and activities. If you wait until you spot some of the more glaring warning signs of drug abuse (e.g., finding marijuana, OxyContin, or a syringe in your son or daughter's backpack), you will have missed the opportunity to catch the problem early on, when your parental influence has a better chance of promoting positive changes in your child's behavior.

At CASA we have spent nearly twenty years identifying the early warning signs of drug use because the sooner you recognize that your teen may be smoking, drinking, using marijuana, or abusing prescription pills or other drugs, the greater chance that you will be able to intervene before drug use escalates to dependence or addiction.

THE SIREN SIGNALS

Some changes in behavior send an alarm that your teen is likely using drugs or alcohol. I call these the Siren Signals. I want you to recognize when changes in your teen's behavior are sending those signals and be prepared to take action. Following are the most common Siren Signals to watch out for and suggestions about what to do.

Dropping Old Friends and Getting New Ones

What adult can keep up with the rapidly changing social life of a teenager? Best friends who spend hours each day texting, talking, and hanging out can become enemies overnight. Relationships and crushes that seemed bigger than life can fizzle in less than a week. Childhood friends may suddenly become uncool, and joining a sports team may cause a shift in social groups. Trying to keep up with your teen's circle of friends can be confounding. But observing the changes and talking to your teen about the reason for the changes can help you distinguish a typical teen shift in friends or activities from a Siren Signal of trouble.

Merely changing friends does not suggest that your child may be drinking or using drugs, but who your child's new friends are might. In a teen's world, friends often reflect one's social identity. New friends can be a good thing; they may reflect a new interest in sports, theater, science, or some other healthy activity. Teens tend to spend their time with other teens who are engaged in similar activities, such as theater, debating, art, music, computer programming, sports—and yes, doing drugs.

Teens who drink or use drugs tend to flock together; they often give up old friends who don't drink or use drugs in favor of new friends who do. If your child's new friends are using substances, it is a Siren Signal that your child may be using too.

If your teen has a new group of friends, try to get to know them. At the very least, find out who the new friends are and talk to your teen about why he or she is hanging out with this new group and what they share in common. If you suspect that these new friends are drinking, smoking, or taking other drugs, discuss your concerns with your teen, reiterate your expectations about not using substances, and monitor your teen's behavior for other Siren Signals. If your teen tells you that her new friends are drinking or using drugs, tell her that she should consider finding others who don't. If she continues to spend time with friends who are a bad influence, you may need to use discipline such as grounding to prevent her from associating with alcohol-drinking and drug-using peers.

Borrowing or Stealing Money

Cigarettes, alcohol, and drugs cost money. Some drugs—a few Vicodin or a fifth of vodka—may be within the weekly allowance of many teens. Other drugs, like ecstasy or cocaine, are more expensive. When smoking, drinking, or drug use becomes frequent, the cost rises faster than Jack's beanstalk.

Teens tend to have limited resources—an allowance or a salary from a part-time job. For most teens, these resources are enough to cover social activities, such as moviegoing or having pizza with friends. But if a teen is using drugs, these resources may start to run out. Teens who have a substance problem may resort to borrowing money (from friends and family members), stealing it, or selling drugs in order to satisfy their own cravings.

Be on the lookout for changes in your child's spending patterns.

Does his allowance suddenly run out before the end of the week? Is she constantly asking you for extra money? Keep track of any cash that you keep in your wallet or around the house so that you notice if money is missing.

Dropping Activities Such as Sports

Sometimes when teens start drinking or using drugs, they lose interest in activities that used to occupy their time, like playing on sports teams, debating, or biking. It may be that the old activities become boring in comparison to partying, or that your child is too tired or out of it to enjoy the activity. Your child's substance use may also be causing a culture clash if the friends who engaged in the old activities disapprove of your child's new behavior.

If your child loses motivation or interest in activities he used to enjoy, find out why. Has your child simply grown out of them? Has he found new activities? If you suspect your child is forgoing productive activities to get drunk or high, you should intervene. Talk to your child about your concerns. Also talk to others in your child's life to find out what they suspect the problem might be. Reengage with your teen; create enjoyable opportunities to spend more time together. If you discover that there is an underlying problem, get your child the necessary help.

Other Common Siren Signals to Look Out For

- Increased secrecy
- Missing or skipping school
- Declining grades
- Constant discipline problems
- Sudden, frequent mood swings
- Aggressiveness
- Irritability

- Depression
- Chronic restlessness
- Sleeping too much or too little
- Difficulty concentrating
- Use of stimulants to study

THE SYMPTOMS OF CURRENT SUBSTANCE USE

Some secrets are easy for kids to keep. You may not notice that your son borrowed the car without your permission. Your daughter may be able to hide the fact that she hooked up with a boy while she and her friends were at the movies. But like Edgar Allan Poe's story, "The Tell-Tale Heart," some secrets are too big to keep hidden, and an observant parent will notice that something is going on.

The behavioral changes described in the previous section indicate that your teenager may be experimenting with or using drugs. However, if your child is actually drunk or high, or is using drugs habitually, there are a set of distinct, clear signs.

Teenagers using drugs will try to hide the evidence from you. But if you know the tell-tale signs, their secret won't be secret very long. Ask yourself questions like these:

- Is your child trying to cover up smells on his or her breath or in his or her room?
- Are controlled prescription drugs missing from your medicine cabinet?
- Is your child using eyedrops to clear red eyes?

The use of each substance is associated with a cluster of unique symptoms, which are described in detail in the "Parent Power Glossary for Parents and Teens" on page 241.

Here are some of the general symptoms that may reveal current drug use:

- Excessive talking, rapid or slurred speech
- Bizarre or paranoid comments
- Excessive forgetfulness
- Difficulty expressing thoughts
- Lack of coordination, poor balance, tipsy walking
- Spaciness, inability to concentrate or follow a conversation
- Bloodshot eyes
- Dilated or very small pupils
- Excessive sweating, jitters, and jumpiness
- Nodding off (eyes closing, head falling forward)
- Nosebleeds, excessively rubbing or wiping the nose
- Constantly popping breath mints, chewing gum, or drinking a flavored drink immediately before talking to you (to cover the smell of alcohol or smoke)
- Missing prescription drugs like OxyContin or Xanax
- Possession of drug paraphernalia such as tin foil, rolling papers, pipes, straws, plastic bags
- Increased accumulation of inhalable products such as glue, hairspray, or nail polish
- Increased accumulation of over-the-counter cold medicine
- Use of incense, room deodorant, or perfumes to hide smoke or chemical odors on clothing or in a room

WHAT TO DO IF YOU SEE
THE SIREN SIGNALS

Early intervention is a potent prevention tool. By being alert to signals that your child may be drinking and using drugs, you can stop the behavior in its early stages. Ending the behavior early significantly reduces the risk that your child's use will lead to harm—an accident, poor school performance, legal problems, brain damage, or addiction.

You are your child's first line of defense. You are uniquely positioned to detect the early signs of drug use. You have the Parent Power and motivation to do something about it.

Think about it. If your son's friends knew that he was smoking pot, would you want to rely on them to tell you? That makes you the best—and perhaps only—chance your child has that someone will intervene and help stop the behavior.

As a parent, you've known your child intimately since birth. You can judge when something is going wrong in your child's life. If you see some of the Siren Signals, or are otherwise worried or suspicious that your child may be smoking, drinking, or using other drugs, there are several steps you can take.

You might start by engaging your inner Sherlock Holmes and investigating the matter further. Ask your child specific questions about

---

Like so many parents, we didn't heed the warning signs. We found an empty beer bottle in the backyard, we smelled pot on his clothes, we found an unidentifiable pill in the laundry room; we chalked these things up to normal teen behavior, but we were wrong. One day, I found his backpack sitting on his bedroom floor, the contents spilling out. Inside was the tie we had given him for Christmas. Only, it was cut in half and he had been using it as a tourniquet. Also in his bag were several bags of heroin and some syringes.

Jim Bildner, whose son died of a heroin overdose; a supporter of Addiction Recovery Management Service (ARMS) at Massachusetts General Hospital in Boston

My then fifteen-year-old son spent a summer periodically using marijuana at a friend's house. I was suspicious, so I called the friend's parent who denied it could be happening in their house. But when the parent asked a younger sibling, she found out it was true.

I talked to both of the boys at our home. I told them how disappointed I was in their behavior, believed they were stronger than that, told them it would stop immediately but they were now going to be under my microscope until they were out of high school, and that I hoped they could rebuild my trust in them by stopping.

Then I talked to my son alone to find out if he was feeling anxious, depressed, or other reasons for why he was using it. He just said they were trying it out (and of course gave all the arguments about how safe and nonaddictive it is, how it should be legal like cigarettes, etc.). I responded by telling him I expect him not to smoke cigarettes either and that no matter what the arguments, pot is still illegal. At the end of a long tearful talk he admitted he wanted to stop because he was sick of losing friends.

Thankfully, in the next few months all those old friends started being around and calling more again, and his friend who had initiated the using came to me in their senior year of high school and thanked me for being stronger than his parents by not just punishing them, but talking about the emotional letdown they had been and giving them the belief that they could be stronger and better kids.

Parent posting on CASA Parent Power discussion forum

his or her activities, friends, and spending habits, and observe your child's response and behavior. The information you collect may confirm or dispel your suspicions.

Follow your intuition if you think there is a problem; your kids may be inclined to lie about their drinking or drug use. Ask probing questions if the things your child tells you don't add up, but be open to the possibility that drugs aren't the root of the problem. In the next section I will discuss what to do if you confirm that your child has started smoking, drinking, or using drugs.

Some suspicious parents choose to search their child's room or possessions, or require their child to take a drug test. As a suspicious parent, you have a right—and it is your job—to search your child's room. A search may turn up evidence of drugs, but if it doesn't, you still can't be sure that your child isn't using. If you conduct a search without your child's permission, your child will likely be angry and will conclude that you don't trust him or her. Tell your child that it is your responsibility to take actions that enable you to protect him and help him lead a healthy, drug-free life; that this is not a matter of not trusting, but of verifying that he is safe and drug free.

"It's None of Your Business"

If your child is an older teen, he may tell you that whether he drinks or uses drugs is none of your business, or that he has the right to decide what he does with his body. If so, you need to establish that as a parent, your child's substance use is your business. Your job is to teach him to make healthy, responsible decisions. You can also stress that as a parent, you need to prevent him from engaging in self-destructive behavior and that drinking and taking drugs can be very dangerous.

Q: If you suspected that your kid was drinking or doing drugs, would you search his or her things (e.g., backpack, clothing, or room)?

A: Yes, I absolutely would go through my child's things. I would also let them know that if I ever suspected anything, that I would have no problem doing it. However, if you do decide to do this, check everywhere and in everything.

A: I have always gone through my son and daughter's personal belongings. Some may call this practice an invasion of their privacy, but this is a great way to know what is going on with your children and their friends.

Parent postings on CASA Parent Power discussion forum
(All parents posting comments answered "Yes.")

WHAT TO DO IF YOUR CHILD IS DRINKING OR USING OTHER DRUGS

Perhaps you noticed that your daughter has a new set of friends and quit the tennis or softball team. When you asked her about it, she admitted that she has been smoking pot on the weekends. Maybe you found some marijuana rolled up in the shade of your daughter's room, or some pills in the pocket of your son's jeans when you were doing the laundry. How should you react?

Though you are not likely to think so at the time, this cloud has a silver lining, because now that you've identified the problem, you can do something about it. As a parent, you can change your child's behavior through ongoing dialogue, setting clear rules, monitoring your child's conduct closely, and enforcing consequences when your child breaks the rules. That's Parent Power in action. Many teens experiment with alcohol, some may experiment with drugs, but most don't go on to develop a substance-abuse problem. How you respond to the discovery of your child's substance use may make a difference between your child stopping it or sinking into trouble.

Discuss Your Concerns with Your Child

If the signs themselves are a problem (e.g., your child is skipping school), or if your investigation suggests that your child is drinking or doing drugs, calmly discuss your concerns directly with your child.

Your conversation will be most effective if you are able to express your concern and disapproval of your child's substance use while also affirming your unconditional love and support: "I notice that your grades are slipping and that you've been sleeping most of the day on the weekends. I'm concerned that something is wrong and I'm worried that you may be doing drugs. I love you and I will help you no matter what the problem is, but I need you to tell me honestly what's going on." You should avoid labeling your child as "bad" or "irresponsible" or a "druggie." Your teen can deal with your condemning his or her mistakes, but if you condemn your child, that child is less likely to respond to your parenting.

The next actions you need to take are to enforce consequences for your child's behavior and to monitor your child closely for signs of continued use.

Enforce Consequences

Hopefully, before you caught your child smoking, drinking, or getting high, you had already talked about substance use. Ideally, in those conversations you discussed your expectations for your child's behavior and the consequences for violating those expectations. If so, and your child has broken the rules, then you should say: "I'm disappointed that you decided to drink [use drugs] and I'm concerned about your safety. I'd like to talk about what happened and why you

Q: If you discovered that your child was drinking alcohol or smoking marijuana or cigarettes, what did you do?

A: First time: Conversation, increased time together as a family, a session with a therapist.

Second time: (involved catching our daughter coming home at 3 A.M., having snuck out of the house at 11 P.M.) Conversation, grounding, weekly Friday night family nights, insistence that she join a sports team (that turned out to have been a great idea), insistence that she join student government at school (another good idea—she met some new friends and felt part of things more).

Third time, two years later: (she turned eighteen, and after two years of no use of drugs/alcohol) She refused to promise she'd not use pot, refused to promise not to keep drug stuff in the house, refused to honor family rules. She left the house and went from friend's house to friend's house for two months, trying to wait us out so we'd let her live at home and smoke/drink as she pleased.

Now, another two years later: She's in rehab for all sorts of junk. She has thanked us for "buying her time" in high school, when she stayed sober.

We'd probably do what we did before, but also bring her for an addiction evaluation after the second time. We'd also probably have gone to Al-Anon ourselves then.

Parent posting on CASA Parent Power discussion forum

did it, and how you plan to avoid doing it again. In the meantime, you know that the consequences for breaking the rule are—you can't use the car [or you're grounded] for a week [month]."

It's important to enforce consequences if you catch your child drinking or using drugs. There's no upside to letting it slide. As I explained in Chapter 1, children need parents to set boundaries so they can establish their own boundaries; children whose parents fail to enforce consequences, or enforce them unevenly, are more likely to abuse substances. Being lackadaisical about your child's behavior will not make you a cool parent and will not help your child learn responsibility or self-control. Instead, your child will get the message that "Anything goes," or "My parents don't care enough to parent me."

If you haven't talked about consequences previously, you can introduce the concept now, but don't worry about finding the perfect solution in the heat of the moment. If you've just found out that your child has been drinking or smoking pot, both you and your child may be upset, angry, or simply not thinking clearly. The better approach is to put off talking about specific consequences until you've had some time to calm down and think about it. In your initial encounter, discuss your concerns about your child's behavior, the risks to his or her health and safety, and mention that there will be consequences: "Your father [or mother] and I are concerned about the fact that you've been drinking [smoking marijuana]. We need to discuss what we think the consequences for your behavior should be. We want you to think about it too, and tomorrow we'll sit down to discuss your behavior and the consequences."

Appropriate consequences might include taking away privileges that matter to your child, for example, grounding, or if your child has a driver's license, taking away driving privileges. Keep in mind that discussing the problem should not be considered a punishment; discussion is a healthy family activity. If you choose to ground your child, don't let her hide in her room watching TV. Try to take advantage of this opportunity to build your relationship with your child. Remember, your child needs parenting, which means she needs you.

Assess the Situation

If you've discovered that your child is smoking, drinking, or using drugs, you need to assess how serious the situation is. Was it a one-time event? Does your child have an underlying problem that needs to be addressed? Is there a history of addiction in your family? You should discuss the situation with your child, but be aware that children who are frequent smokers, drinkers, or marijuana users are more likely to lie about it.

You should also determine, with professional help if necessary, whether your child is struggling with other issues, such as depression, anxiety, or stress, that need to be addressed. If you are unsure whether

---

Caught in the Act

Your daughter comes home from a party, reeking of alcohol, and runs into the bathroom to throw up. You come home early from work one night and find your son smoking pot on the porch.

What should you do?

Wait until your child is sober to talk about it. Having a rational conversation with a teenager can be difficult enough, but nearly impossible if she or he is drunk or high. This doesn't mean that you should ignore what's going on. If she is sick, take care of her; if he is stoned, tell him, "I don't want to talk to you about this while you're high, we'll discuss it tomorrow morning."

---

your child just tried a drug once or is using regularly, have your child evaluated by a professional.

Monitor Your Child Closely

Once you find out that your child has started using, you need to monitor your child more closely; be on the lookout for the Siren Signals of use, and for lying that may signal your child continues using. If your child is going to a party at a friend's house, call the friend's parents to check that they will be home and there will be no alcohol or drugs available. Set a curfew and enforce it. Make it a habit to wait up for your kids when they return home after going out. Talk to them

---

Should you be home drug testing? It comes down to a very personal and individual decision, and there is no clear or easy answer to this question. The home drug tests are not perfect, and there are risks associated with the testing process, but if you don't think you can keep your kids safe any other way, then maybe home drug testing is worth doing. If your child does have a history of drug use or substance-abuse problems, then the arguments towards testing get a lot more compelling, and if your child has a history of lying to you about their substance use, then you may not need to worry much about eroding your trust relationship.

If you do decide that you need to test your child, make sure you have a reasoned talk with them explaining why you're doing it, and explaining that you are testing them only because you love and worry for them. Parenting teens is a tough job, and there are rarely easy answers.

Parent posting on CASA Parent Power discussion forum

---

before they go to bed. If your child knows that she has to look you in the eye, talk to you, and kiss you goodnight, she is not likely to drink or smoke pot. Keeping close tabs will keep your kid safe.

Some parents make their children take regular drug tests. You should speak to a doctor, psychiatrist, or counselor if you think that drug testing might be necessary or appropriate for your child.

Seek Professional Advice

If you discover or suspect that your child is drinking or using drugs regularly, consult someone who can help you to assess the problem, such as your child's doctor, a therapist, a school counselor, or your priest, minister, or rabbi. Your child may be more likely to open up and accept help from someone who is not in a position of authority and to whom he or she can speak confidentially. Physicians, clergy, and school counselors aren't necessarily trained to deal with substance-abuse problems, but those who are may be able to judge the severity of the problem. Those who aren't may be able to recommend a professional who can provide screening and, if necessary, treatment. If you don't know who to talk to, your local Al-Anon or Alateen chapter may be able to point you in the right direction. Simply call their national hotline (888-4AL-ANON or 888-425-2666) and explain that you're concerned about your child's drug or alcohol use.

WHAT TO DO IF YOUR CHILD IS ADDICTED TO ALCOHOL OR OTHER DRUGS

Learning that your child is addicted to any substance is heartbreaking. At this point, both you and your child need help in dealing with the problem. As a parent, you should seek support and counseling for yourself; professional counselors and support groups such as Al-Anon,

Alateen, or parenting support groups in your community can help you to deal with your own emotions, provide assistance in obtaining treatment for your child, and put you in a better position to help your child.

Addiction is a serious disease, and you should address finding treatment as you would any other serious medical problem. Research your options. Find the best treatment provider for your child. Unfortunately, it can be very difficult to find professional drug- or alcohol-treatment programs for children. Even if you're fortunate enough to have insurance that covers substance-abuse treatment, there may not be science-based, effective, and affordable treatment programs for children and teens in your area.

There are people in your community who may be able to help you find a treatment program for your child. Ask your pediatrician or family doctor, friends and family members. Look on your medical insurance company's website or call your local Al-Anon, Alcoholics Anonymous, or Narcotics Anonymous chapter and ask for a referral. Don't give up–keep calling.

Another useful tool for finding an appropriate treatment program for your child is SAMHSA's Substance Abuse Treatment Facility Locator, an online U.S. government system that allows you to identify treatment options by city and state. The website address is findtreatment.samhsa.gov. You can call their toll free number: 800-662-HELP. You might be able to get help finding an appropriate treatment program through your state's health department; many states have set up toll-free hotlines for people seeking help for a substance-abuse problem.

Your child may not respond to your attempts to get him or her to stop using. Don't despair. Don't blame yourself. Don't give up. Get help. Continue to be engaged and stay in touch with your child.

In the last meal I had with my close friend and partner Edward Bennett Williams, when the legendary criminal lawyer was close to death, I asked him, "What's the most important thing you've ever learned?"

"Always leave a light in the window. For the kids. So they know they always have a home to come to whatever happens to them, whatever they've done."

Addiction is a chronic disease, and its treatment, even successful treatment, often entails relapse. Given the ravaging effects the disease has on family members, supporting your child through treatment can be painfully difficult. Reach out to others for support and never give up. Always leave a light on in the window for your child.

Acknowledgments

This book is a collaborative effort, grounded in almost twenty years of research at The National Center on Addiction and Substance Abuse (CASA) at Columbia University, the nation's premier institution in the field, as well as my experiences as secretary of Health, Education, and Welfare in the Carter administration, Lyndon Johnson's top domestic affairs aide, and New York State Governor Hugh Carey's special counsel on drug and alcohol abuse.

It is in good measure shaped by the hard work of Elizabeth Planet, CASA vice president and director of special projects, and Emily Feinstein, one of CASA's finest researchers. These talented young women have not only devoted untold hours to research and interviews, but they have been with me through endless drafts of the manuscript. This book is a much better product because of their ingenuity, dedication, and determination to make it a practical, usable guide to help parents raise healthy, substance-free children. Elizabeth Planet has been a star at CASA for seven years; Emily for a year. Both are in the early stages of public service that will make significant contributions in this complex field of substance abuse, and in pursuit of social justice.

I am greatly indebted to those who read early drafts of all or part of this manuscript. Their insights and suggestions have enriched this book.

A number of experts and clinicians (many parents among them) read the entire manuscript: Linda C. Barr, MD, assistant clinical professor of psychiatry, Yale School of Medicine; Claudia Califano, MD, resident in psychiatry at Yale-New Haven Hospital; Peggy Collins, a perceptive reporter and writer; Herbert D. Kleber, MD, professor of psychiatry and director, Division on Substance Abuse at Columbia University and the New York State Psychiatric Institute, and one of the nation's top experts in substance abuse; Ralph Lopez, MD, clinical professor of pediatrics, Weill Cornell Medical College, author and extraordinary physician specializing in adolescent medicine; James Rao, LMSW, Mount Sinai Adolescent Health Center; Jeanne Reid, a doctoral candidate and former CASA researcher; David Rosenbloom, PhD, CASA president and CEO; Susan Foster, CASA vice president and director of Policy Research and Analysis; and Jon Morgenstern, PhD, CASA vice president and director of Health and Treatment Research and Analysis.

Roy J. Bostock, MBA, chairman, Partnership for a Drug-Free America, and a former trustee of Duke University; Rev. Edward (Monk) Malloy, president emeritus, University of Notre Dame; and Manuel Pacheco, PhD, past president, University of Missouri System and University of Arizona, reviewed the chapter "How Can I Prepare My Kids for College?"

Nicholas A. Pace, MD, clinical associate professor of medicine at New York University Medical Center, and CASA senior researchers Aaron Hogue, PhD, and Charles Neighbors, PhD, reviewed the "Parent Power Glossary for Parents and Teens."

Many thanks to Edward Klaris, Leigh Montville, and the cartoonists at the *New Yorker* magazine, as well as Rob Rogers and Steve Kelley for donating the cartoons sprinkled throughout this book.

The Gordie Foundation, which works to educate college students to avoid the dangers of alcohol, binge drinking, peer pressure, and hazing, provided financial support that helped make this book possible.

Tamara Schlinger, CASA's general counsel, acted as my agent with great skill and commitment to this undertaking.

CASA librarian David Man, PhD, MLS, library research specialist Barbara Kurzweil, and CASA researcher Varouj Symonette helped with the critical fact-checking.

Kathleen Ferrigno, CASA's director of marketing, and Lauren Duran, CASA's director of communications, have been working hard on plans to make parents aware of how this book can help them raise healthy, drug-free children.

As usual, Jane Nealy helped with the manuscript, JoAnn McCauley kept me reasonably on schedule during this process, and Sue Brown kept the administrative wheels at CASA turning.

The Touchstone/Fireside team at Simon and Schuster have been superb: my editor Michelle Howry, publisher Mark Gompertz, editor in chief Trish Todd, publicity director Marcia Burch, and associate publisher Chris Lloreda.

Several people helped with ideas for the cover design: Kenny Evans, group creative director, Gotham Inc. (whose contribution of talent and time was made possible by Michael I. Roth, chairman and chief executive officer of Interpublic), and Cherlynne Li, the Fireside art director who did the final cover.

I owe special thanks to my wife, Hilary, who (once again) lived through the many weekends, early mornings, and late evenings I spent in the spectacular study she has created for me in Westport, Connecticut. She is the love of my life and has been for more than a quarter century, during which she has showered me with love, sage advice, and her spectacular sense of humor.

I am indebted to all of the above; this book would not be possible without them. But responsibility for what's on these pages rests on my shoulders alone.

JAC, Jr.
June 2009

Parent Power Glossary for Parents and Teens

COMMONLY USED TERMS

Addiction is a chronic, relapsing disease characterized by compulsive drug seeking, cravings, and continued use despite harm. The social consequences of addiction include low academic achievement, troubled interpersonal relationships, unemployment or underemployment, and isolation.

Dependence occurs when a user develops a tolerance to a drug and suffers withdrawal when the drug is discontinued. The terms "addiction," "dependence," and "alcoholism" are interchangeable—they are all characterized by a progressive lack of control over one's drug use.

Drug means nicotine, alcohol, illegal drugs, prescription drugs, and over-the-counter and toxic substances, such as inhalants.

Substance refers to any drug, such as nicotine, alcohol, illegal drugs, prescription drugs, and toxic substances, such as inhalants.

Substance Abuse is using a drug in spite of the negative legal, health, and safety consequences, and/or the inappropriateness of the drinking/drugging experience.

Tolerance describes 1) the amount of a drug a person can ingest without feeling or showing the drug's effects (for example, the ability to drink a few beers and not get drunk) and 2) the brain's response to prolonged use of a drug in such a way that it accommodates larger amounts of the drug (over time, the user will need more of the drug to feel the same effects).

Withdrawal is the syndrome of often painful physical and psychological symptoms that occurs when a person stops taking a drug.

CIGARETTES AND TOBACCO

What are cigarettes and tobacco?

Tobacco is made from the dried leaves of a plant that contains many chemicals, including nicotine. Tobacco comes in several forms:

- Cigarettes and cigars are made by rolling tobacco leaves in paper. Tobacco companies add other chemicals to cigarettes, some of which have been linked to cancer.
- Dip, chew, and pipe tobacco are forms of pure tobacco that are sold in tins. Rolling tobacco is sold in pouches and is used to hand roll cigarettes.

What do cigarettes and tobacco do?

Cigarettes contain stimulants that increase the heartbeat and blood pressure. The most important stimulant is called nicotine. Some users experience a mild euphoria or rush after smoking and a feeling of stress relief. Smoking may decrease the appetite.

Young smokers frequently report symptoms such as wheezing,

shortness of breath, coughing, and an increase in phlegm production. In general, teen smokers have a greater susceptibility to colds and flus than nonsmokers.

How are cigarettes and tobacco used?

Cigarettes and cigars are the most popular form of tobacco. Cigarettes are inhaled into the lungs; cigars are not meant to be inhaled. The chemicals from the tobacco make their way into the user's blood stream. Some people also put a pinch of tobacco directly into their mouth and hold it in their cheek so that the chemicals can be absorbed through the lining of the mouth and cheek.

What other names do people use for cigarettes and tobacco?

Beedi, Camel, cancer stick, chew, cig, ciggy, dip, fag, looseys, smoke, snuff, and stoge/stogie.

What are the signs of use?

Signs of smoking include the smell of smoke on your child's clothing, skin, or hair, yellowing of the teeth, wheezing or shortness of breath, and a persistent cough.

How bad is it? What are the long term side effects?

Tobacco use is a leading cause of death in the United States. Cigarette smokers have an increased risk for heart disease, blood clots, cancer, strokes, bronchitis, emphysema, bad circulation, and ulcers. Cigar and pipe smokers and chewing tobacco users are at higher risk of developing cancers of the mouth and neck.

Teenagers who smoke are much more likely to be addicted to cigarettes as adults. A child who makes it to twenty-one before trying her first cigarette is virtually certain not to become addicted later in life. Teenagers who have never smoked cigarettes are also unlikely to try other drugs, including marijuana and cocaine.

How addictive is it?

Cigarettes are highly addictive, due to the nicotine found in tobacco. Some experts consider nicotine to be more addictive than heroin. People who start smoking before the age of twenty-one find it very hard to quit later in life.

ALCOHOL

What is alcohol?

The oldest and most widely used drug in the world, alcohol is also the drug most frequently used by teens. More likely than not, your child has or will try it.

Alcohol is a distilled liquid that is made from fruits, grains, and vegetables. The most common forms of alcohol are beer, wine coolers, malt beverages, wine, and liquor (e.g., bourbon, gin, scotch, and vodka). Alcohol companies also make sweet, teen-friendly drinks and market them to your children. Sometimes called alcopops, these drinks include Mike's Hard Lemonade, Smirnoff Ice, and Zippers, which are prepackaged Jello-shots.

The concentration of alcohol in each of these beverages differs; beer has the lowest percentage of alcohol, wine has slightly more, and liquor has the most alcohol. In the U.S., one twelve-ounce bottle of beer, one five-ounce glass of wine (about a half cup) and one 1.5-ounce shot of liquor have the same amount of alcohol. Alcopops often have more alcohol than beer.

What does alcohol do?

Drinking can seriously affect your teenager's judgment, reaction time, and coordination. Alcohol works by depressing the central nervous system, affecting motor coordination, reflexes, visual, and other sensory perceptions and emotions. It can relax the drinker and reduce social inhibitions.

Teenagers who drink too much may become confused or depressed, have short-term memory loss, and may vomit or pass out. Teenagers who drink large amounts of alcohol in a short period of time can develop alcohol poisoning, a potentially life-threatening condition.

How is alcohol used?

Alcohol is a liquid that people drink. Some teenagers prefer to mix liquor with soda, juice, or some other beverage that disguises the smell and taste of the alcohol. Adolescents who want to get drunk will often drink shots, which are small glasses of straight liquor, because the body absorbs the alcohol much faster that way.

What other names do people use for alcohol?

Booze, brew, brewskies, cold one, juice, sauce, hooch, cocktail, moonshine, and vino.

What are the signs of use?

Signs of teenage drinking include the smell of alcohol on your child's breath, slurred speech, lack of coordination, nausea, vomiting, and hangovers.

How bad is it? What are the long-term side effects?

Drinking can physically damage the developing brains of teenagers in ways that impair learning, memory, abstract thinking, problem solving, and perceptual-motor skills (such as eye-hand coordination). Drinking at an early age can interfere with social and behavioral development, interrupt academic progress, increase the chance of risky sexual behavior, and increase the risk of serious injury and death. Heavy drinking also increases the risks of cirrhosis of the liver and other liver diseases, like heart disease and breast cancer, later in life.

Teen drinking and driving can be fatal; car crashes are the leading cause of death in the U.S. for teenagers and alcohol is a major factor in a quarter of those deaths.

Teenage drinking can also lead to more serious substance-abuse problems. Kids who start drinking regularly before age fifteen are more likely to develop alcoholism than those who start drinking at twenty-one. Almost all adults who are addicted to alcohol began drinking before the age of twenty-one. Teenagers who binge drink (i.e., in one sitting, for boys, five or more drinks; for girls, four or more drinks) are more likely to use illicit drugs than teens who don't.

How addictive is it?

Alcohol can be psychologically addictive, which means that the user feels like they need to drink in order to feel good, deal with life, or cope with stress. In addition, frequent users of alcohol or those with certain genetic traits can develop a tolerance to the drug. Heavy drinking can lead to physical dependency (i.e., addiction). Withdrawal from alcohol can be painful and even life-threatening. Symptoms of alcohol withdrawal range from shaking, sweating, nausea, anxiety, and depression to hallucinations, fever, and convulsions.

MARIJUANA

What is marijuana?

Marijuana is the most popular illicit drug among teens. It comes from a plant called Cannabis sativa and looks like a dry, shredded, greenish-brown herb. Each part of the plant—the flowers, stems, seeds, and leaves—can be used to get high. The main active chemical ingredient in marijuana is THC (delta-9-tetrahydrocannabinol).

What does marijuana do?

Marijuana affects the pleasure receptors in the brain the same way as other drugs like tobacco, alcohol, heroin, and cocaine. It causes a hazy euphoria, or high, often called being stoned. Some people experience pleasant sensations. For example, colors and sounds may seem more intense. Marijuana can also cause anxiety, paranoia, distrust, panic, and depression. It also causes temporary cognitive defects, including short-term memory loss and shortening of attention span.

How is marijuana used?

Marijuana is usually smoked. It can be rolled in paper and smoked like a cigarette (called a joint), rolled in a cigar that has been emptied of tobacco (called a blunt), smoked out of a pipe or smoked out of a water pipe (called a bong). Marijuana can also be mixed in or cooked in food (e.g., brownies) or brewed as a tea.

What other names do people call marijuana?

Bud, chronic, dope, ganja, grass, herb, hydro, indo, mary jane, pot, sinsemilla, skunk, reefer, and weed.

What are the signs of use?

Signs of marijuana use include dry mouth, red or bloodshot eyes, pungent smell on clothing, skin, or hair, short-term memory gaps, excessive giggling, hunger (munchies) or thirst, and impaired reaction time. Other signs of use include burning incense or using other deodorizers to cover the smell, frequent use of eyedrops, and owning paraphernalia, such as pipes and rolling papers.

How bad is it? What are the long-term side effects?

The effects of marijuana are particularly damaging for the developing minds of adolescents. Marijuana can impair critical cognitive functions related to attention, memory, and learning, the effects lasting up to twenty-four hours or more after use. Using marijuana at a time when these skills are particularly important for succeeding in school may cause children to fall behind in their intellectual, emotional, and psychological development. Withdrawal from marijuana also causes symptoms such as restlessness, irritability, and sleep disturbance that can interfere with learning and other activities.

Someone who smokes marijuana regularly can develop the same respiratory problems that tobacco smokers do, including a persistent cough, an increased risk of colds, flu, and lung infections, and an increased risk of cancer of the respiratory tract and lungs.

Marijuana use may lead to other drug use. Although most kids who use marijuana will not move on to harder drugs, twelve- to seventeen-year-olds who smoke marijuana are much more likely to use cocaine than those who do not.

How addictive is it?

Marijuana can be addictive. Frequent users of marijuana can develop a higher tolerance. Marijuana users may become dependent upon it to feel good, deal with life, or handle stress. Because their brains are still developing, adolescents who use marijuana are more likely to become dependent on it than adults, and the younger the child starts using, the more likely that child is to become addicted.

INHALANTS

What are inhalants?

Kids can use everyday products that they find in their homes to get high. Inhalants are carbon-based substances like glue, aerosol gases, lighter fluid, cleaning fluids, and paint products that when inhaled produce effects similar to alcohol or anesthetics. Inhalants are popular among younger (twelve- to sixteen-year-old) teens. They are readily available, relatively cheap, and are legal for kids to buy.

What do inhalants do?

Inhalants act on the central nervous system (CNS), slowing the body's functions, including heart rate and breathing. In small doses, inhalants create a feeling of intoxication similar to alcohol. In large doses, inhalants can produce psychoactive, or mind-altering, effects. The effects do not last long—only a few minutes to an hour at most.

An overdose will cause disorientation, loss of control, and even unconsciousness, although the user generally recovers quickly. When using some products (particularly aerosol gases and cleaning fluids), a prolonged sniffing session can cause irregular and rapid heartbeat and even lead to heart failure and death. So-called sudden sniffing death can result from a single session of inhalant use. However, such deaths are rare.

How are inhalants used?

The product is inhaled or sniffed to get high. Some kids try to intensify the effect by sniffing the product from inside of a bag placed over the head, which is extremely dangerous.

What other names do people use for inhalants?

Air blast, ames, amys, boppers, bullet, buzz bomb, glue, hardware, heart-on spray, huff/huffing, laughing gas, moon gas, oz, pearls, poppers, quicksilver, rush, snappers, snotballs, whippets, and whiteout.

What are the signs of use?

Signs of inhalant use include dizziness, drunk or dazed appearance, and missing household items.

How bad is it? What are the long-term side effects?

Chronic use of inhalants can cause serious damage to the brain, heart, lungs, liver, and kidneys. In rare cases, abuse of inhalants can be fatal.

How addictive is it?

Children who use inhalants regularly may develop a tolerance to them and some users become psychologically dependent on them. Most children do not use inhalants for more than a short period of time, but some continue to use them for several years.

STEROIDS

What are steroids?

Anabolic steroids (steroids) are manufactured drugs that mimic the naturally occurring male hormone testosterone. When anabolic steroids are abused for athletic or cosmetic purposes, they can have dangerous side effects.

Anabolic steroids are distinguished from corticosteroids, which have no abuse potential, and are used to treat conditions such as asthma, chronic lung disease, skin conditions, and allergic reactions.

What do steroids do?

Steroids increase muscle mass, strength, and endurance, and reduce body fat. People generally use steroids to improve performance or appearance.

Because steroids act like hormones, they affect men and women differently.

- Women who use steroids can develop excessive body and facial hair, male-pattern baldness, a deepening of the voice, shrinking of the breasts, menstrual irregularities, and genital swelling.
- Men may experience baldness, breast enlargement, sterility, impotence, shrunken testicles, difficulty or pain in urinating, and increased risk for prostate cancer.

Other physical effects include liver tumors, jaundice, water retention, and high blood pressure.

In addition, steroids can cause severe emotional and cognitive side effects, including uncontrolled aggression and violent behavior, severe mood swings, manic episodes, depression, paranoia, jealousy, extreme irritability, and even delusions.

How are steroids used?

Tablets or liquid forms are generally swallowed, but steroids can also be injected. Combining different steroids to intensify their effect is called stacking.

What other names do people use for steroids?

A's, anabolics, arnies, balls or bulls, gym candy, juice, pumpers, roids, stackers, and weight trainers.

What are the signs of use?

Signs of steroid use include rapid weight gain or muscle development, acne flare-up, fluid retention, yellow tint in the eyes and skin (jaundice), mood swings, such as depression or aggressive behavior, and premature balding.

How bad is it? What are the long-term side effects?

Steroids can have a magnified effect on teenagers since their bodies are still growing. Teen use of steroids can result in stunted growth, which is permanent.

Over time, steroid buildup can become toxic to the body and lead to hypertension, high cholesterol, kidney disease, and heart damage.

How addictive is it?

Steroid use can lead to psychological and physical dependence. When teens stop taking steroids, the withdrawal can be severe, causing depression, uncontrollable rage, delusional and suicidal thinking, and paranoid psychosis.

OVER-THE-COUNTER DRUGS
CONTAINING DXM

What are over-the-counter drugs?

Over-the-counter cold and cough medicines are sold without a pre-scription. Some contain the cough-suppressing ingredient called dex-tromethorphan (DXM), which creates a high when taken in large doses. There are many different products that contain DXM, includ-ing Robitussin, Dayquil, and some Vicks products; often these prod-ucts have "Tuss" or "DM" in their name.

What does DXM do?

If taken in large quantities, DXM can cause hallucinations, loss of motor control, and out-of-body (or dissociative) sensations.

Side effects of excessive cold and cough medicine use include fever, confusion, impaired judgment, blurred vision, dizziness, paranoia, ex-cessive sweating, slurred speech, nausea, vomiting, abdominal pain, irregular heartbeat, high blood pressure, headache, lethargy, numb-ness of fingers and toes, dry and itchy skin, loss of consciousness, seizures, brain damage, and even death.

How are over-the-counter drugs used?

Cough and cold medicines, which come in tablets, capsules, gel caps, and lozenges as well as syrups, are swallowed in large doses to achieve intoxication. DXM can also be extracted from cough and cold medi-cines, turned into a powder, and snorted.

What other names do people use for over-the-counter drugs?

Candy, c-c-c, dex, DM, drex, red devils, robo, robotripping, rojo, triple c, tussin, velvet, and vitamin D.

What are the signs of use?

Signs of cold or cough medicine abuse include missing medicine or empty medicine containers, intoxication, lethargy, spaciness, slurred speech, and redness of face.

How bad is it? What are the long-term effects?

Excessive use of DXM can produce hallucinogenic and other psychiatric effects and can lead to brain damage and death.

How addictive is it?

Regular and ongoing use of cough and cold medicines can lead to psychological dependence.

PAINKILLERS (OPIOIDS)

What are painkillers?

Opioids are strong prescription painkillers used by doctors to treat serious and chronic pain. Commonly abused painkillers include OxyContin, Vicodin, fentanyl, Darvon, Dilaudid, codeine, Demerol, Percoset, and Percodan. Opioids are derived from or are structurally related to morphine.

Between 1992 and 2003, the incidence of first-time uses of painkillers among teens increased an astounding 542 percent, more than four times the rate of increase among adults.

What do painkillers do?

Painkillers attach to the opioid receptors in the brain, blocking the transmission of pain signals. They may produce a quick, intense feeling of pleasure, which is followed by a calm drowsiness, and feelings of relaxation and contentment.

Painkillers also cause drowsiness, inability to concentrate, apathy, lack of energy, constipation, nausea, vomiting, and, most significantly, respiratory depression.

How are painkillers used?

Painkillers are typically sold as pills that are meant to be swallowed but can also be crushed up and inhaled (snorted). Some painkillers come in liquid form and can be injected.

What other names do people use for painkillers?

Blue, china white, hillybilly heroin, hydro, kicker, norco, OC, oxy, OX, oxies, oxycotton, percs, pills, vikes, and 80s.

What are the signs of use?

Signs of use include constricted pupils, slow reaction time, haziness in thinking, missing medicine bottles, change in appetite and sleeping patterns, shallow breathing, constipation, and nausea.

How bad is it? What are the long-term side effects?

When used for nonmedical purposes, painkillers can alter brain activity and lead to dependence and addiction. Taking a large dose of opioids at one time, or mixing them with alcohol or other drugs, can cause severe respiratory depression and death.

How addictive is it?

Prescription opioids, like their illicit counterpart heroin, are addictive. However, some painkillers are more addictive than others. The strongest dose painkillers, such as OxyContin, have the highest potential for addiction. Opioid withdrawal symptoms include insomnia, flulike symptoms, bone and muscle pain, diarrhea, and vomiting.

STIMULANTS (UPPERS)

What are stimulants?

Stimulants are prescription drugs that physicians use to treat asthma, respiratory problems, obesity, attention deficit/hyperactivity disorder (ADHD), and sleep disorders like narcolepsy. The most commonly abused stimulants are Ritalin, Adderall, and Dexedrine.

What do stimulants do?

Stimulants excite the central nervous system. They may cause euphoric effects, and help people stay awake and focus. They cause feelings of exhilaration, energy, and increased mental alertness. Teenagers often take stimulants to stay awake, boost energy, get high, or as a study aid to increase alertness and concentration.

Side effects include increased heart rate, blood-pressure rate, and metabolism, jitters, rapid or irregular heartbeat, reduced appetite, weight loss, heart failure, dilated pupils, loss of coordination, dizziness, tremors, headache, chest pain with palpitations, excessive sweating, vomiting, abdominal cramps, feelings of restlessness and anxiety, delusions, hostility and aggression, panic, and suicidal or homicidal tendencies. Paranoia, often accompanied by auditory and visual hallucinations, may also occur. Stimulants can cause heart attacks in patients with underlying cardiac disease (e.g., high blood pressure).

How are stimulants used?

Stimulants are pills that are meant to be swallowed. The pills can also be crushed up and the snorted or mixed with alcohol. Teenagers who are prescribed stimulants for ADHD can save up their pills and share them with friends or sell them.

What other names do people use for stimulants?

Bennies, black beauties, crosses, dexies, hearts, LA turnaround, rippers, ritz, speed, truck drivers, uppers, and vitamin R (Ritalin).

What are the signs of use?

Look for signs of alertness, increased energy or attention span, excessive talking, anxiety, or decreased appetite.

How bad is it? What are the long-term side effects?

Stimulants can alter brain activity and lead to dependence. Withdrawal symptoms may include depression, disturbance of sleep patterns, fatigue, and apathy.

How addictive is it?

Stimulant use can lead to tolerance and addiction.

DEPRESSANTS (DOWNERS)

What are depressants?

Depressants are used by doctors to treat anxiety and sleep disorders. Commonly prescribed depressants include barbiturates such as phenobarbital, Nembutal (pentobarbital) or Seconal, and benzodiazepines such as Valium (diazepam), lorazepan, temazepam, and Xanax.

What do depressants do?

Depressants slacken the central nervous system (CNS), causing slower breathing and a general sense of relaxation, reduced pain and anxiety, a feeling of well-being, and lowered inhibitions.

Side effects include impaired coordination, memory, and judgment, respiratory depression, sensory depression, fatigue, confusion, and irritability. Psychological side effects include poor concentration or feelings of confusion, and lowered inhibitions. Barbiturates may also cause sedation, drowsiness/depression, unusual excitement, fever, irritability, poor judgment, slurred speech, and dizziness.

The effects of depressants can be dangerously intensified by mixing them with alcohol.

How are depressants used?

Tranquillizers are pills that are swallowed.

What other names do people use for depressants?

Barbs, downers, jellies, sekkies, sleepers, temazies, tranx or tranks, and V's.

What are the signs of use?

Signs of depressant use include dilated pupils, slurred speech, relaxed muscles, intoxication, dizziness, sedation, drowsiness, and fever.

How bad is it? What are the long-term side effects?

When used for nonmedical purposes, depressants can alter brain activity and lead to dependence; they can be fatal when taken in large quantities or when mixed with other drugs.

Long-term use of some depressants has been associated with increased aggression, significant depression, memory problems, cerebral atrophy (brain shrinkage), decreased motivation, irritability, impaired sexual functioning or menstrual irregularities, weight gain, sleep disorders, emotional disinhibition, and rage.

How addictive is it?

Depressants are physically and psychologically addictive. Users may quickly develop a tolerance to depressants. Withdrawal from some depressants can be serious and life-threatening.

ECSTASY (MDMA)

What is ecstasy?

Ecstasy is a designer, man-made drug that is chemically similar to the stimulant methamphetamine and to the hallucinogen mescaline. Many ecstasy pills contain additional drugs or drug combinations that can be harmful, including methamphetamine, caffeine, dextromethorphan (DXM), the diet drug ephedrine, and methylenedioxyamphetamine (MDA).

What does ecstasy do?

MDMA acts both as a stimulant and a psychedelic, producing an energizing effect and intensifying emotions, as well as creating distortions in time and perception, and enhancing enjoyment from tactile experiences (touch). The effects generally last four to six hours.

Short-term effects include feelings of mental stimulation, emotional warmth, enhanced sensory perception, and increased physical energy.

Side effects can include nausea, chills, sweating, teeth clenching, dry mouth, muscle cramping, and blurred vision.

Many ecstasy users experience depression, paranoia, anxiety, and confusion. There is some concern that these effects on the brain and emotions can become permanent with chronic use of ecstasy.

Because MDMA can interfere with the body's ability to metabolize and excrete the drug, taking a lot of the drug within short intervals can create potentially harmful levels in the body (i.e., overdose). Ecstasy also raises the temperature of the body. This increase can sometimes cause organ damage and, in rare but unpredictable circumstances, death.

How is ecstasy used?

Ecstasy comes in powder, tablet, or capsule form. It is usually swallowed in the form of a powder-filled capsule or a pill. The powder can be snorted. It is considered a party drug, and is often used at concerts, raves, and other music-oriented parties. Adolescents and young adults also use ecstasy in social settings (e.g., house parties) because it creates feelings of closeness and empathy, and reduces inhibitions.

What other names do people use for ecstasy?

Adams, beans, disco biscuit, E, go, hug drug, rolls/rolling, X, and XTC.

What are the signs of use?

Signs of use include teeth clenching, dilated pupils, chills or sweating, and excessive displays of affection.

How bad is it? What are the long-term side effects?

Research using animals has shown that ecstasy can cause long-term damage in the parts of the brain that are involved in mood, thinking, verbal memory, and judgment.

Many people suffer mild to severe withdrawal symptoms after using the drug, including fatigue, loss of appetite, depressed feelings, and trouble concentrating.

How addictive is it?

Ecstasy has not been proven to be physically addictive; however, teenagers who use it can become psychologically dependent upon it to feel good, deal with life, or handle stress.

LSD (ACID)

What is LSD?

Lysergic acid diethylamide (LSD) is a man-made hallucinogen that was popularized in the 1960s as a mind-expanding drug. It is an odorless and colorless substance with a slightly bitter taste. It is usually found in the form of liquid, or tablets, capsules, or "tabs." Tabs are pieces of blotter paper that have absorbed liquid LSD and have been divided into small squares, each square representing one dose.

What does LSD do?

LSD affects neurotransmitters in the brain, including dopamine, serotonin, and glutamate, in areas that are associated with sensory stimulation and emotion.

The psychedelic effects of LSD vary depending on the amount taken, the mood the person is in, and the user's surroundings. Reported psychedelic experiences include intensified colors, distortion of vision and hearing, heightened self-awareness, mystical or ecstatic experiences, and a sense of being outside one's body. Hallucinations and delusions, such as believing that something exists when it does not, are rare, although they may occur at higher doses. Some users experience unpleasant reactions (a bad trip), including feelings of depression, dizziness, disorientation, fear, paranoia, and panic. Physical side effects include dilated pupils, higher body temperature, increased heart rate and blood pressure, sweating, loss of appetite, sleeplessness, dry mouth, and tremors.

Deaths due to suicide or overdose are rare but can occur.

How is LSD used?

LSD is ingested orally.

What other names do people use for LSD?

Acid, blotters, doses, dots, hits, microdots, sugar cubes, tabs, and trips.

What are the signs of use?

Signs of use include dilated pupils, strange behavior or conversation, and paranoia.

How bad is it? What are the long-term side effects?

There is strong evidence that some healthy adolescents who use LSD will develop schizophrenia or severe depression as a result. It is not clear how LSD triggers these illnesses or who it will happen to.

LSD users can experience flashbacks, during which part of the LSD experience can reoccur, even if the user stopped taking the drug days, months, or years before. These flashbacks may be disorienting and even dangerous, depending on when they occur (e.g., while driving).

How addictive is it?

There is no evidence that LSD is physically addictive, although users can develop a short-term tolerance to the drug.

METHAMPHETAMINE (METH)

What is methamphetamine?

Methamphetamine is an illicit drug, found most commonly in the Midwest and Western states. It is a highly addictive form of speed that is often cheaper and easier to find than heroin or cocaine.

Almost all methamphetamine is homemade and resembles a white to yellowish fine or coarse powder, crystal, or chunks. It is sold in small plastic bags or wraps, aluminum foil, capsules, or tablets of various sizes and colors.

What does methamphetamine do?

Methamphetamine is a long-acting stimulant. People who take it experience feelings of euphoria, heightened alertness, and greater energy. Like other stimulants, the drug increases the heart rate and breathing, sometimes creating heart palpitations. Methamphetamine is a powerful appetite suppressant.

As the drug wears off, people often experience feelings of extreme fatigue or depression.

The physical side effects of long-term use also include hair loss, tooth loss, and loss of the ability to think clearly.

How is methamphetamine used?

Methamphetamine is a powder that can be injected, inhaled (snorted), smoked, or swallowed.

What other names do people use for methamphetamine?

Chalk, chicken feed, chris, christy, crank, crystal, crystal meth, glass, go-fast, ice, meth, shabu, speed, trash, tweak, yaba, yellow yam, and zip.

What are the signs of use?

Signs of methamphetamine use include dilated pupils, rapid speech followed by slurred speech, disturbed sleep patterns (staying up late, sleeping for long periods), nervous physical activity, jitteriness, decreased appetite, and excessive weight loss. Meth-related paraphernalia includes straws, rolled-up dollar bills, razor blades, pipes, and burnt aluminum foil.

How bad is it? What are the long-term side effects?

Excessive or long-term use of methamphetamine may cause long-term damage to the part of the brain associated with emotions and pleasure. Chronic use reduces the user's ability to feel pleasure—from anything. Other consequences of long-term use include paranoia, anxiety, mood and sleep disorders, and violent behavior. Heavy use can lead to coma, stroke, or death.

How addictive is it?

Methamphetamine is highly addictive.

COCAINE

What is cocaine?

Cocaine is a stimulant that is derived from the coca plant. Powder cocaine is a purified form of the drug that is sold in most large and midsize cities. Crack cocaine is made by cooking cocaine powder with baking soda and water to form a concentrated solid substance (rocks).

What does cocaine do?

Like other stimulants that affect the central nervous system, cocaine can produce feelings of euphoria or well-being, mental exhilaration, reduced appetite, great physical strength and mental capacity. It can also cause jitteriness, anxiety, paranoia, and panic. Cocaine raises the heart rate, and in large amounts can cause heart failure. While it is rare, some first-time users of even small amounts of cocaine can experience heart failure and/or sudden death.

How is cocaine used?

Cocaine powder is usually inhaled (snorted), but it can also be smoked or injected. Crack is smoked from a pipe.

What other names do people use for cocaine?

Blow, Charlie, coke, flake, nose candy, perico, rock, ski/skiing, snow, and tornado.

What are the signs of use?

Signs of cocaine use include dilated pupils, excessive talking, nosebleeds, anxiety, or paranoia. Cocaine-related paraphernalia includes straws, rolled-up dollar bills, razor blades, and mirrors with white residue.

How bad is it? What are the long-term side effects?

The long-term health effects of cocaine include addiction, heart attacks, respiratory failure, strokes, and seizures. Chronic cocaine abuse can lead to premature death, permanent paranoia or psychosis, and damage to structures of the nose.

With long-term abuse, the brain loses its capacity to experience pleasure without the drug.

How addictive is it?

Cocaine is highly addictive.

HEROIN

What is heroin?

Heroin is a highly concentrated derivative of morphine, which is extracted from the poppy plant.

Heroin is typically sold in small bags and looks like a white or brownish powder. Sometimes it comes in the form of a black sticky substance called black tar.

What does heroin do?

Heroin enters the brain quickly and binds with the opioid receptors, slowing down cognitive functions, reaction time, and memory. Short-term effects include a surge of euphoria followed by feelings of calm or contentedness, drowsiness, and cloudy mental functioning.

The concentration of heroin varies widely from dose to dose, so users are always at risk of an overdose (especially if the drug is injected). Heroin overdose is fatal if not treated immediately.

How is heroin used?

Heroin can be injected, smoked, or inhaled (snorted). Before the 1990s, people needed to inject the drug to get high because the product was so impure. Starting in the 1990s, high-purity forms of heroin became widely available. Snorting or smoking the high-purity form creates an intense high without using needles.

What other names do people use for heroin?

Big H, black tar, brown sugar, dope, H, horse, junk, mud, skag, and smack.

What are the signs of use?

Signs of heroin use include constricted pupils, drowsiness, nodding off, impaired mental functioning, slowed-down respiration, nausea/vomiting, reduced appetite, slurred speech, and scars at injection sites ("track marks"). Heroin paraphernalia includes straws, rolled-up dollar bills, razor blades, pipes, burned aluminum foil, tourniquets, hypodermic needles, and burnt spoons.

How bad is it? What are the long-term effects?

The risks of heroin use include overdose (death) and addiction. Chronic use can lead to infections of the heart lining and valves, cellulites, and liver disease. Heroin's depressant effect on breathing increases the risk of contracting certain lung diseases, like pneumonia.

Heroin withdrawal is painful; symptoms include severe restlessness, muscle and bone pain, insomnia, chills, sweats, diarrhea, vomiting, and other intense flulike symptoms.

How addictive is it?

Heroin is highly addictive.

OTHER DRUGS OF ABUSE

There are more drugs available to your children than you could imagine, and every year, new drugs are added to the list. Here is a brief description of some of the other drugs your child may be exposed to.

GHB. GHB (gamma hydroxybutyrate) is an odorless and tasteless liquid made from industrial chemicals. It is classified as a sedative and has long-lasting euphoric effects on the user. GHB may be used as a date-rape drug because of its relaxing effect and its ability to impair judgment and memory—victims who were given GHB often forget the details surrounding a sexual assault. GHB overdose can be fatal.

Hashish. Similar to marijuana, hashish is derived from the cannabis sativa plant. It is a THC-rich resinous material that is dried and compressed into hard shapes (e.g., balls). Pieces of hashish are broken off, placed in a pipe, and smoked.

Ketamine. Ketamine (K, special K, vitamin K) is an animal tranquilizer that is used by veterinarians. Ketamine became popular as a recreational drug because of its powerful hallucinogenic and dissociative effects—it impairs perceptions, creates feelings of euphoria, and distorts the user's sense of time and place. Ketamine comes in a powder or liquid form. Side effects include delirium, amnesia, damage to the motor system, and potentially fatal respiratory problems.

Mushrooms. Magic mushrooms or 'shrooms are wild mushrooms that contain the hallucinogenic chemicals psilocybin and psilocin. When eaten (fresh, cooked, or dried), mushrooms create hallucinogenic experiences similar to LSD, but milder. Side effects may include vomiting, nausea, and stomach pains. As with other hallucinogenic drugs, users can have an unpleasant trip or experience a psychotic episode.

Methadone. Methadone is a synthetic analgesic (developed to replace morphine) that is used medically as a treatment for heroin addiction. It is available in oral solutions, tablets, and as an injectable liquid. Chronic methadone use leads to addiction, and is associated with prolonged withdrawal syndrome.

Opium. Opium is derived from the poppy plant and is a relative of morphine. It is sold as a dark, sticky, tarlike substance and is generally smoked from a pipe, but can also be injected. Like all opioids, opium is addictive.

PCP. Phencyclidine (PCP, angel dust, ozone) is a powerful anesthetic. Users feel euphoric and spacey but may also experience acute anxiety, paranoia, violent hostility, and, in some cases, a psychosis indistinguishable from schizophrenia. PCP comes in a white crystalline powder that is often smoked but can be snorted or injected. It has a strong chemical smell, similar to ammonia. Overdose can lead to suicidal and hostile behavior, coma, convulsions, and possibly death (from respiratory arrest).

Peyote/Mescaline. Peyote is a small cactus that contains the hallucinogenic ingredient mescaline. Peyote has been used by some Native American cultures as a part of religious rituals. Mescaline can be extracted from peyote or produced synthetically. The long-lasting hallucinogenic effects are intensely visual; side effects include anxiety, racing heart, dizziness, diarrhea, vomiting, headache, bad trips, and possible psychosis.

Rohypnol. Rohypnol (roofie) is a powerful tranquilizer. Rohypnol pills can be swallowed, or crushed and dissolved in drinks—the effects are similar to the intoxication of alcohol, plus sedation. The drug gained notoriety as the date-rape drug because of its combined sedative effect and its ability to literally erase the user's memory. The drug may be fatal if taken in excess or combined with alcohol.

Salvia. Salvia divinorum is a powerful herbal hallucinogenic, also known as diviner's sage. Salvia can be chewed, smoked, or taken as a tincture. The effects last for only a few minutes and range from uncontrollable laughter to intense hallucinations or delusions. Some users experience unpleasant or uncomfortable feelings. Salvia can be purchased over the Internet, although it has been outlawed in several states.

Parent Power Reference List for Parents and Teens

For more information about the topics covered in this book, and to connect with experts and other parents, please visit www.Straight DopeForParents.org.

To access research and policy reports from The National Center on Addiction and Substance Abuse (CASA) at Columbia University, please visit www.CASAcolumbia.org.

To participate in Family Day, please visit www.CASAFamilyDay .org.

The following resources may be of particular interest to you and your family.

Drug Facts/Drug Policy

American Legacy Foundation: www.americanlegacy.org

American Medical Association Office of Alcohol and Other Drug Abuse: www.ama-assn.org/ama/pub/category/3337.html

Join Together at CASA, A Service of The National Center on Addiction and Substance Abuse at Columbia University: www.jointogether.org

National Institute on Alcohol Abuse and Alcoholism (NIAAA): www.niaaa.nih.gov

National Institute on Drug Abuse (NIDA): www.drugabuse.gov

Office of National Drug Control Policy (ONDCP):
www.whitehousedrugpolicy.gov

The Partnership for a Drug-Free America: www.drugfree.org

U.S. Drug Enforcement Administration: www.usdoj.gov/dea

Parent and Community Organizations

American School Counselor Association: Tips and resources to prepare children for middle school and high school. www.schoolcounselor.org

Children Now, Talking with Kids About Tough Issues: Tips for parents on how to talk to children aged eight to twelve about sex, HIV/AIDS, violence, drugs, and alcohol. www.talkingwithkids.org

CollegeDrinkingPrevention.gov: Information on issues related to alcohol abuse and binge drinking among college students; look up university drug and alcohol policies. www.collegedrinkingprevention.gov/policies

Community Anti-Drug Coalitions of America (CADCA): Supports community coalitions in their efforts to create drug-free communities. 800-54-CADCA or www.cadca.org

Leadership to Keep Children Alcohol Free: Helps parents prevent the use of alcohol by children ages nine to fifteen. www.alcoholfreechildren.org

Mothers Against Drunk Driving (MADD): Information about the dangers of teen drinking, including drinking and driving. www.madd.org

National Parent Teacher Association (PTA): Connect and chat with other parents, find after-school programs for your children, and learn how you can volunteer. www.pta.org

Parents Helping Parents (PHP): Example of a community organization that provides support and services to parents of children abusing alcohol or other drugs. www.parentshelpingparents.info

Parents. The Anti-Drug: Federal government website that provides parents with advice and tools to raise drug-free kids. www.theantidrug.com

The Partnership for a Drug-Free America: www.drugfree.org, or go directly to the Parent Tool Kit, www.drugfree.org/parent/home

Princeton Review: Provides information for parents and teens about colleges, including which ones are party schools. www.princetonreview.com/college

Substance Abuse and Mental Health Services Administration (SAMHSA) Center for Substance Abuse Prevention: Provides prevention tools for communities and families. preventionplatform.samhsa.gov

Mental Health Organizations

American Academy of Child and Adolescent Psychiatry (AACAP): www.aacap.org

Federation of Families for Children's Mental Health: www.ffcmh.org

Substance Abuse and Mental Health Services Administration (SAMHSA), National Institutes of Health: www.samhsa.gov

Treatment, Recovery, and Support Groups

Al-Anon/Alateen: Support for people who have a friend or relative with a drinking or drug problem. 888-4AL-ANON (888-425-2666) or www.al-anon.org

Alcoholics Anonymous (AA): Support for people who want to stop drinking. 212-870-3400 (see phone book for local listing) or www.aa.org

American Cancer Society: Free phone-based programs to help people quit smoking. www.cancer.org

Faces and Voices of Recovery: An advocacy organization for persons in recovery. www.facesandvoicesofrecovery.org

Narcotics Anonymous (NA): Support for people who want to stop using drugs. 818-773-9999 (ext. 771) or www.na.org

SAMHSA Substance Abuse Treatment Facility Locator: 800-662-HELP or 800-ALCOHOL (Alcohol Treatment Referral Hotline) or findtreatment.samhsa.gov/facilitylocatordoc.htm

The American Legacy Foundation: Free online smoking-cessation program. www.becomeanex.org

Bibliography

American Council for Drug Education. "Facts About Drugs." www
.acde.org/parent/Research.htm (accessed February 6, 2009).

Califano Jr., Joseph A. *High Society: How Drug Abuse Ravages America and What to Do About It.* New York: Public Affairs, 2007.

CASA. *Dangerous Liaisons: Substance Abuse and Sex,* 1999.

CASA. *Family Matters: Substance Abuse and the American Family,* 2005.

CASA. *Food for Thought: Substance Abuse and Eating Disorders,* 2003.

CASA. *Malignant Neglect: Substance Abuse and America's Schools,* 2001.

CASA. *National Survey of American Attitudes on Substance Abuse: Teens and Parents,* 1995–2008.

CASA. *Non-Medical Marijuana III: Rite of Passage or Russian Roulette?* 2008.

CASA. *So Help Me God: Substance Abuse, Religion and Spirituality,* 2001.

CASA. *Substance Abuse and Learning Disabilities: Peas in a Pod or Apples and Oranges?* 2000.

CASA. *The Commercial Value of Underage and Pathological Drinking to the Alcohol Industry,* 2006.

CASA. *The Formative Years: Pathways to Substance Abuse,* 2003.

CASA. *The Importance of Family Dinners,* 2003, 2005–2007.

CASA. *Tobacco: The Smoking Gun,* 2007.

CASA. *Under the Counter: The Diversion and Abuse of Controlled Prescription Drugs in the U.S.,* 2005.

CASA. *Wasting the Best and Brightest: Substance Abuse at America's Colleges and Universities,* 2007.

CASA. *Women Under the Influence.* Baltimore: The Johns Hopkins University Press, 2006.

CASA. *You've Got Drugs V,* 2008.

Centers for Disease Control and Prevention. "Involvement by young drivers in fatal alcohol-related motor-vehicle crashes: United States, 1982–2001." *Morbidity and Mortality Weekly Report* 51(2002): 1089–91.

Chambers, R. Andrew, et al. "Developmental neurocircuitry of motivation in adolescence: A critical period." *American Journal of Psychiatry* 160(2003): 1041–52.

Colliver, J. D., et al. *Misuse of prescription drugs: Data from the 2002, 2003, and 2004 National Surveys on Drug Use and Health* (DHHS Publication No. SMA 06-4192, Analytic Series A-28). Rockville, Maryland: Substance Abuse and Mental Health Services Administration, Office of Applied Studies, 2006.

Crews, Fulton, Jun He, and Clyde Hodge. "Adolescent cortical development, a critical period of vulnerability for addiction." *Pharmacology, Biochemistry and Behavior* 86(2007): 189–99.

Eaton, Danice K., et al. "Youth Risk Behavior Survey—United States, 2007." *Morbidity and Mortality Weekly Report* 57(2008):1–131.

Freitas, Donna. *Sex and the Soul: Juggling Sexuality, Spirituality, Romance, and Religion on America's Campuses.* New York: Oxford University Press, 2008.

Hirschfelder, A. B. *Encyclopedia of Smoking and Tobacco.* Phoenix: Oryx Press, 1999.

Jacobsen, L., et al. "Impact of Cannabis Use on Brain Function in Adolescents." *Annals of the NY Academy of Sciences* 1021(2004): 384–90.

Kaiser Family Foundation. "National Survey of Adolescents and Young Adults: Sexual Health Knowledge, Attitudes and Experiences." 2003. www.kff.org/youthhivstds/3218-index.cfm (accessed February 6, 2009)

Ketcham, Katherine, and Nicholas A. Pace. *Teens Under the Influence: The Truth About Kids, Alcohol and Other Drugs—How to Recognize the Problem and What to Do About It.* New York: Ballantine Books, 2003.

Kindlon, Dan. *Too Much of a Good Thing.* New York: Hyperion, 2001.

Lopez, Ralph I. *The Teen Health Book: A Parent's Guide to Adolescent Health and Well-Being.* New York: W.W. Norton and Company, Inc., 2003.

Lubman, Dan I. "Substance use and the adolescent brain: A toxic combination?" *Journal of Psychopharmacology.* 21(2007): 792–94.

Martin, C. A., Kelly, T. H., et al. "Sensation seeking, puberty and nicotine, alcohol and marijuana use in adolescence." *Journal of American Academy of Child and Adolescent Psychiatry.* 41(2002): 1495–1502.

National Council for Drug Education. "Signs and Symptoms of Drug Use." www.acde.org/parent/signs.htm (accessed February 6, 2009).

National Institute of Drug Abuse. "Drugs, Brains, and Behavior—the Science of Addiction." 2007. www.nida.nih.gov/scienceof addiction/brain.html (accessed February 6, 2009).

National Institute on Alcohol Abuse and Alcoholism. *Alcohol Alert 73: Underage drinking—highlights from the Surgeon General's call to action to prevent and reduce underage drinking.* Rockville, Maryland: U.S. Department of Health and Human Services, October, 2007.

National Institute on Alcohol Abuse and Alcoholism. "Alcohol and the Developing Adolescent Brain." 2008. www.niaaa.nih.gov/ NR/rdonlyres/87033E59-822F-4491-B0B5-F08C7C955588/0/ NIAAA_Brain_Fact_Sheet_508.pdf (accessed February 6, 2009).

National Research Council and Institute of Medicine. *Reducing Underage Drinking: A Collective Responsibility.* Edited by R. J. Bonnie and M. E. O'Connell. Washington, D.C.: National Academies Press, 2004.

Office of National Drug Control Policy, National Youth Anti-Drug Media Campaign. "Keeping Your Teens Drug-Free: A Family Guide." www.theantidrug.com/pdfs/resources/general/General_Market_Parent_Guide.pdf (accessed February 6, 2009).

Office of National Drug Control Policy. "Drug Facts." www.whitehousedrugpolicy.gov/drugfact/index.html (accessed February 6, 2009).

Office of National Drug Control Policy. "Street Terms." www.whitehousedrugpolicy.gov/streetterms/default.asp (accessed February 6, 2009).

Office of the Surgeon General. *Preventing tobacco use among young people: A report of the Surgeon General.* Washington, D.C.: U.S. Government Printing Office, 1994.

Partnership for a Drug-Free America. "Partnership Attitude Tracking Survey (PATS)—Parents 2008 Report." 2009. www.drugfree.org/Files/new_pats_survey_2008 (accessed February 6, 2009).

Partnership for a Drug-Free America. "Time to Talk." www.timetotalk.org/Downloads/ttt_drug_chart.pdf (accessed February 6, 2009).

Pemberton, M. R., et al. "Underage Alcohol Use: Findings from the 2002–2006 National Surveys on Drug Use and Health" (DHHS Publication No. SMA 08-4333, Analytic Series A-30). Rockville, Maryland: Substance Abuse and Mental Health Services Administration, Office of Applied Studies, 2008.

Schwebel, Robert. *Saying No Is Not Enough.* New York: Newmarket Press, 1998.

Substance Abuse and Mental Health Services Administration. *Results from the 2007 National Survey on Drug Use and Health: National*

Findings (Office of Applied Studies, NSDUH Series H-34, DHHS Publication No. SMA 08-4343). Rockville, Maryland, 2008.

TeensHealth. "Drugs: What You Should Know." www.kidshealth .org/teen/drug_alcohol/drugs/know_about_drugs.html (accessed February 6, 2009).

The Center on Alcohol Marketing and Youth at Georgetown University (CAMY). "Television: Alcohol's Vast Adland." December, 2002. camy.org/research/tv1202/TVbrochure-english.pdf (accessed February 6, 2009).

The Center on Alcohol Marketing and Youth of Georgetown University (CAMY). "Youth Exposure to Alcohol Advertising on Television, 2001 to 2007." 2008. www.camy.org/research/tv0608/ (accessed February 6, 2009).

U.S. Drug Enforcement Administration. "Drug Information." www .usdoj.gov/dea/concern/concern.htm (accessed February 6, 2009).

U.S. Drug Enforcement Administration. Just Think Twice website. "Drug Facts." www.justthinktwice.com/factfiction/Marijuanais harmless.cfm (accessed February 6, 2009).

Volkow, Nora, and Ting-Kai Li. "Drugs and alcohol: treating and preventing abuse, addiction and their medical consequences." *Pharmacology & Therapeutics* 108(2005): 3–17.

Volkow, Nora. "Keynote Address." Presented at CASA conference, "Double Jeopardy: Substance Abuse and Co-Occurring Mental Health Disorders in Young People." October 18, 2007.

Volkow, Nora, et al. "Dopamine in drug abuse and addiction: results from imaging studies and treatment implications." *Molecular Psychiatry* 9(2004): 557–69.

Zeigler, D. W., et al. "The neurocognitive effects of alcohol on adolescents and college students." *Preventive Medicine.* 40(2005): 23–32.

About the Author

JOSEPH A. CALIFANO, JR., was born on May 15, 1931, in Brooklyn, New York, where he grew up. He received his Bachelor of Arts degree from the College of the Holy Cross in 1952, and his LLB from Harvard Law School in 1955. After service in the U.S. Navy and three years with Governor Thomas Dewey's Wall Street law firm, he joined the Kennedy administration and served in the Pentagon as general counsel of the army and as Secretary of Defense Robert McNamara's special assistant and top troubleshooter.

President Lyndon Johnson named Mr. Califano his special assistant for domestic affairs in 1965, and he served in that post until the president left office in January 1969. During his years on the White House staff, Mr. Califano worked on the Medicare and Medicaid programs, and helped shape dozens of Great Society bills related to health care, education, children, criminal justice, the environment, consumers, and social welfare. The *New York Times* called him "Deputy President for Domestic Affairs." At the end of his term, President Johnson wrote to Mr. Califano, "You were the captain I wanted and you steered the course well."

From 1969 to 1977, Mr. Califano practiced law in Washington, D.C., and served as attorney for the *Washington Post* and its reporters Bob Woodward and Carl Bernstein, *Newsweek*, and others during the Watergate years.

From 1977 to 1979, Mr. Califano was U.S. secretary of Health, Education, and Welfare and became the first voice to alert the nation to the explosion of health-care costs and teenage pregnancy, mounted the first national antismoking campaign, began the computer policing of Medicare and Medicaid to eliminate fraud and abuse, issued the first Surgeon General's Report on Health Promotion and Disease Prevention, *Healthy People*, to set health goals for the nation, and instituted Medicare reimbursement for hospice care and financed construction of the nation's first freestanding hospice in Branford, Connecticut. As secretary, he issued federal regulations to provide equal access for handicapped Americans, and Title IX regulations to provide equal opportunity for women in college athletics.

From 1979 to 1992, Mr. Califano practiced law in Washington, D.C.

In 1992, he founded The National Center on Addiction and Substance Abuse (CASA) at Columbia University, where he has served as chair and president and devoted his life to combating substance abuse and addiction, especially among children and teens. CASA is the only national organization that brings together under one roof all the professional disciplines needed to study and combat all types of substance abuse as they affect all aspects of society. CASA and its staff of more than fifty professionals have issued numerous reports and white papers, published books, conducted demonstration programs focused on children, families, and schools at 224 sites in 87 cities and counties in 34 states, Washington, D.C., and two Native American reservations. CASA has held 18 conferences attended by professionals and others from 49 states, and has been evaluating the effectiveness of drug and alcohol treatment. CASA is the creator of the nationwide initiative *Family Day—A Day to Eat Dinner with your Children*™, celebrated on the fourth Monday in September, to promote parental engagement as a simple and effective way to reduce children's risk of smoking, drinking, and using illegal drugs.

Mr. Califano has been adjunct professor of health policy and management at Columbia University's Medical School and School of Public Health. He is a member of the Institute of Medicine of the National Academy of Sciences.

Mr. Califano is the author of eleven previous books (two with Howard Simons, former managing editor of the *Washington Post*) and has written articles for the *New York Times,* the *Washington Post,* the *Wall Street Journal, Reader's Digest,* the *New Republic, America,* the *New England Journal of Medicine,* and other publications. He is married to Hilary Paley Byers and lives in Westport, Connecticut. He has three children, Mark, Joseph III, and Claudia; two stepchildren, Brooke Byers and John F. Byers IV; and eight grandchildren.

Index